MOMENTS O

Twelve Twentieth-Century Women Writers

Lorna Sage was professor of English at the University of East Anglia and twice dean of the faculty. She regularly reviewed for the *Observer*, *London Review of Books*, *Times Literary Supplement* and *New York Times Book Review*. Her previous books include *Women in the House of Fiction* (1992), *The Cambridge Guide to Women's Writing in English* (1999), a short monograph of Angela Carter, and *Bad Blood*, which was the winner of the 2000 Whitbread Biography Award. She died in January 2001.

For more information on Lorna Sage, visit
www.4thestate.com/lornasage

MOMENTS OF TRUTH

Twelve Twentieth-Century Women Writers

Lorna Sage

With an Introduction by Marina Warner

FOURTH ESTATE • *London*

This paperback edition published in 2002
First published in Great Britain in 2001 by
Fourth Estate
A Division of HarperCollins*Publishers*
77–85 Fulham Palace Road,
London w6 8jb
www.4thestate.com

10 9 8 7 6 5 4 3 2 1

A catalogue record for this book is available from the British Library

ISBN 1-84115-636-1

Typeset by Palimpsest Book Production Limited,
Polmont, Stirlingshire
Printed in Great Britain by
Clays Ltd, St Ives plc

CONTENTS

AUTHOR'S NOTE

This book's centre of gravity is pre-war, complementing *Women in the House of Fiction*, on postwar women novelists (1992). The title alludes to the modernist 'epiphany' (the kind of revelatory denouement one of its major subjects, Katherine Mansfield, was so expert at and addicted to in her stories); and to a different kind of realisation, the moment when each writer discovered her voice, found her calling or failed to, or remade herself as an author en route. It echoes, too, Woolf's phrase, 'Moments of Being', but the stress here is more on *doing*, writing as work.

Sometimes I'm looking at people's first books (Woolf's *The Voyage Out*, Stead's *The Salzburg Tales*), at other times at their only major work (Barnes's *Nightwood*, Bowles's *Two Serious Ladies*), or at the books that made the difference to their fortunes, as with Carter's *Bloody Chamber* and *Sadeian Woman*, both published in 1979. The unifying theme is the meaning of vocation. Edith Wharton, describing her 1899 debut, wrote; 'thereafter I never questioned that story-telling was my job . . . I felt like some homeless waif who after trying for years to take out naturalisation papers and being rejected by every country, has finally acquired a nationality. The Land of Letters was henceforth to be my country.' Her Parisian exile completed her 'naturalisation' in her new homeland.

However, others of the writers here never found themselves a home: Violet Trefusis, for example, bitterly echoed the title of Wharton's autobiography, *A Backward Glance*, when she called her own memoir (which suppressed the most important facts of her life, in particular her love-affair with Vita Sackville-West) *Don't Look Round*. Trefusis mocked her own talent, and is mainly now remembered as a character in others' books. She wrote a dissenting *roman à clef*, *Broderie anglaise*, to tease Woolf and Vita, but it was in French, and it seems that neither of them read it. Her writing is sardonically lightweight, accomplished and comic, as in *Hunt the Slipper*, discussed here. 'You'll only *play* at being free and bohemian . . .' she'd written to Vita: a true prophecy for herself, too.

Jean Rhys – who, unlike Trefusis, needed to work for money – dramatised in *After Leaving Mr Mackenzie* the dizzying and unlikely emergence of an artist's model and kept woman into bleak self-awareness. The setting, again, is Paris. It was Rhys's first truly confident and original novel – though it owed a lot to Mansfield's example. Jane Bowles in 1943 in *Two Serious Ladies* produced a one-off work that still more or less defies labels – it 'never *was* a novel', she realised – but at least she did, marvellously, produce it, though later she became hopelessly blocked and convinced that 'I am isolated and my experience is probably of no interest . . . to anyone.' She's in good company, however. Djuna Barnes in the 1930s had hilariously bemoaned the many ways in which *Nightwood* failed to fit the novelistic bill: 'they all say that it is not a novel; that there is no continuity of life in it, only bright spots and poetry – that I do not give anyone an idea of what the persons wore, ate or how they opened and closed doors, how they earned a living . . .'

Originality had a cost. Barnes was often hailed as a genius, sometimes by herself – 'my talent is my character, my character my talent, and both an estrangement'. But genius, especially when attributed to women writers (Emily Brontë was the examplar) exiled them in singularity. And in any case it was becoming a doubtful notion. Christina Stead stages a debate on the question among her story-tellers: the Centenarist (a publicist) argues that it is 'a matter of chance whether real talent is chosen or trampled under in the mud', the writers who survive are not necessarily the best or the most 'universal'. And perhaps there are no such creatures anyway. Stead in her own voice years later, in a 1968 essay called 'The Ocean of Story', talked of 'the million drops of water that are the looking-glasses of all our lives'. Everyone has a story. Christine Brooke-Rose, experimental novelist and critic, would criticise in a similar spirit the priestly exclusiveness of the avant-garde canon, even when it proclaimed the death of the author. However, there is another angle on this question, addressed in literary biography: Barnes's *Nightwood* would probably never have been published without the mediation of her self-appointed reader, literary agent and editor Emily Coleman, who persuaded Barnes to finish the book, and T. S. Eliot at Faber to publish it. On the evidence, great modernist works were produced out of dialogue, they weren't the cloned brain-children of 'genius'.

Simone de Beauvoir wrote in *The Second Sex* 'One is not born a genius, one becomes a genius', a suggestive variation on her much more famous remark that one is not born a woman but becomes one. *The Second Sex* is the only work of non-fiction covered in the book, but it is read here as a kind of anti-novel, devoted to demolishing myths about feminine character and destiny. Beauvoir's radical suspicion of fictions and representations was derived in large part from her reading of women writers, and links her with new novelists and experimenters. It also means that the creation of herself in the character of a writer becomes her major project – her life's work is her life, living and writing converge. She thus pushes to an extreme a strain found in other writers here: Katherine Mansfield, whom she quotes often; also Jean Rhys, whom she doesn't, but who nonetheless stages scenes that strikingly anticipate existentialist studies in bad faith. And after Beauvoir, Iris Murdoch's first fiction is inspired in part by her battle with utopian anti-art, a sort of imaginative civil war in which she is on both sides, but comes down in favour of illusionist practice against theory. Traditional artists are better at picturing consciousness, Murdoch argued, than abstract thinkers.

There are many such connections, some unexpected, among the dozen writers discussed in these essays. For instance, there is a recurrent evolutionary theme, starting with Darwinian echoes in Wharton and Woolf, surfacing again in Rhys, Stead and Barnes (who imagines her circus performers with their *déformations professionnelles* as mutants, and whose shocking final scene has a woman on all fours with a dog), through to Carter and the wolfish metamorphoses of *The Bloody Chamber*. Other cross-associations are fluid and fishy: Murdoch catches a common vision of regeneration when she writes lyrically that 'Each human being swims in a sea of faint suggestive imagery. It is this web of pressures, currents and suggestions . . . which ties our fugitive present to our past and future.'

Together, the individual pieces collected in *Moments of Truth* compose a group portrait of the woman artist in the last century.

Lorna Sage, 2000

OPEN QUESTIONS

An Introduction by Marina Warner

The word 'glamour' comes from grammar, and Lorna Sage, who combined wit and panache with a scathing dislike of sloppiness, embodied this paradox to the full.[1] In her now classic memoir, *Bad Blood*, she tells us how, when she began learning Latin, she instantly loved it, could do it, wanted to use it; language was a refuge, and the place she wanted to be was in her head, with literature her companion. So she was grammatical – and she had glamour.

Lorna Sage's thinking about writing affected a whole generation of writers, publishers and, not least, readers. It's difficult to communicate how exhilarating it was to be read by her, to be the object of her attention, to be spared her satirical wit, and win her praise – to be *rated* by her. It first happened to me with my second novel, *The Skating Party*. Terence Kilmartin, a great friend of hers, for whom she regularly wrote some of her deftest criticism at a vintage time for the *Observer*'s literary pages, suddenly confided that she had been eloquent on the book's behalf on a prize they were judging. News of her interest in it came as a real parting of the rain clouds. She was interested in me, and, as it did for others who were lucky enough to be in this position, this interest fired me up, made my writing feel worthwhile.

But Lorna was never cosy: her partisanship was tempered by irony, and words like malicious, cackling, mocking, freakish, profane, figure in her vocabulary of praise. She finessed a rare position: she cultivated the English literary talents of scorn and scepticism and utopian bile without becoming a rancid Swiftian; her misanthropy was lightened by humour, by glee, by genuine, infectious pleasure. Certain moods of melancholy, certain bleak and ghastly states were meat and drink to her; she used the phrase 'cosmic irony' about Edith Wharton, and the concept wasn't a stranger. She valued 'a good hater'. Yet, at the same time, she had a rare laugh: a wonderful, rich, deep complicit chuckle, which came readily bubbling up, even when she was suffering atrocious effects of illness.

In the major extended essay about Simone de Beauvoir included here, Lorna Sage wonders: who is Beauvoir speaking for? Whom or what does she *own* – own in the sense of acknowledge as her own. Thinking about postwar feminism and *The Second Sex*, Lorna puzzled over, not the mirage of matriarchal lineage, but the possibility of owning and owning up to another constituency, which was female in gender, feminine in practice, applicable generically to the enterprise of living as a woman, inside and outside texts, yet respectfully particular in every individual case. With Angela Carter, her close friend, ally, comrade-in-arms and fellow sufferer – from human folly as well as shortness of breath – she wanted to reconfigure the 'we' women could use. They were, both of them, profoundly impatient with claims to niceness and motherliness, to goddess revivals and myths of 'wimmin'. Angela Carter provocatively co-opted the Marquis de Sade to her quest for female freedom;[2] Lorna Sage, coincidentally, was looking for its polymorphous possibilities elsewhere, in women who wrote. They both wanted to forge a new kind of 'Us'.

This collection of essays about twelve women writers was sifted from her spirited and prodigal output by Lorna before she died in January 2001; she discusses Edith Wharton, Jean Rhys and Jane Bowles, among others, concluding with her friends, Iris

Murdoch, Angela Carter and Christine Brooke-Rose. Introductions to reprints of classic works such as Virginia Woolf's *The Voyage Out*, and Katherine Mansfield's short stories, combined with longer journal articles, shape her incisive, original take on the interplay between text and person, between the life and the work; the reader can watch Lorna Sage's thinking through the all-important twentieth-century relationship of memoir and invention, record and fabrication.

Lorna Sage began a life in criticism as an advocate of postmodern fabulism, exemplified by the playful allusiveness and textual games of Italo Calvino in *The Castle of Crossed Destinies*, Angela Carter in *Nights at the Circus*, Umberto Eco in *The Name of the Rose* and Christine Brooke-Rose in her nimble, witty metafictions. Her critical sensors were tuned by days and nights and years of continual, voracious, scrupulously fine reading: at her memorial service in April 2001, Victor Sage, her first husband, recalled with dry wit marathon sessions during which Lorna would, for example, 'do Scott', that is, read the entire oeuvre of Sir Walter Scott, one book after another, including titles long forgotten. Lorna was hyperacutely calibrated to the way a book lies – in more senses than one. As a critic, she's alert to the unspoken resonances between lines, and the wider rings of thought spreading beyond them. She continually startles her readers with the sensitivity of her attentiveness to implication, to the ellipses in her chosen subjects' sentences, to the way she hears the full chord, and its harmonic overtones, not the single notes and can follow their reverberations. In a tribute to Angela Carter after her death in 1992, for example, she quotes Angela reminiscing about her brother and her younger self, wondering how 'such camp little flowers as ourselves emanated from Balham via Wath-upon-Dearne . . .' Lorna takes the thought and, with characteristic verve, places it far beyond Angela's slightly defensive self-mockery, on the vertiginously larger, subtler, emotional map of *Zeitgeist* and literature after Modernism, when she comments, 'This is not about nostalgia but connects with a quite different contemporary sensation: of coming at the end, mopping up, having the freedom of anomie.'[3]

In the 1990s, when she was writing these essays, Lorna was responding to the rise of the genre now widely referred to as 'life-writing' with a fresh set of questions and rereadings of writers whom she already knew well. Memoirs, confessions, testimony, diaries and even travel journals were swelling the category, beyond all expectation, in the decades following the proclaimed 'Death of the Author'. Barthes's celebrated essay had become a manifesto for a critical generation, but far from disappearing from the text, the author was rising, like the indestructible undead, and haunting literature far and wide, blurring the boundaries between fact and fiction, memory and imagination. Autobiography was displacing the novel, it seemed, as the prime literary vehicle of human experience. The work of W. G. Sebald, for example, one of Lorna Sage's colleagues at the University of East Anglia, cannot be classified along any former lines: the stories in *The Emigrants* and *The Rings of Saturn*, though aesthetically highly fictional in tone and execution, are convincingly recounted as events in the life of the writer, posited as genuine memories. At the same time, readers hunger to know if a story is true, and they respond differently to the play of the author's presence between the lines if they can be persuaded this is the person to whom this really happened. As Adam Phillips has remarked, 'Today we value truthfulness, not truth.'[4]

Lorna had a special reason besides to want to probe the territory where fiction meets memory: she was writing her own memoirs. Some brilliant early instalments of *Bad Blood* had memorably appeared in the *London Review of Books* years before she managed to finish the book, which wonderfully revealed her literary gifts to a much wider public. *Bad Blood* is extraordinarily evocative, richly remembered, brave, very funny, sharp, poignant, gallant, packed with character – and characters – an adventure story of reckless youth, experiment and escape. She lived to see its success: the *Daily Telegraph* reviewer said it 'encapsulates the experience of a generation. This is not just an exquisite personal memoir, it is a vital piece of our collective past.' Mary Beard, reviewing in the *Times Literary Supplement* wrote that the description of Valma's attempts 'to make gravy is one of the best accounts of domestic melodrama that I have ever read'. It was a surprise best seller, and won the Whitbread Prize for Biography. Telling the story of her family and upbringing, Lorna shows us – and we need reminding – that literature really can make something happen: books here became her voyage out, her forged papers out of a childhood hell. She was such a scalpel-sharp reader and such a fierce advocate of certain writing because she saw that literature and language are catalysts in the making of experience, not simply passive precipitates.

Bad Blood draws on the remarkable diary kept by her wicked grandfather, the 'Old Devil', the philandering vicar, of his days and nights, his ups and downs. Lorna wanted him to get into print, perhaps because he had called her after a heroine from a book – Lorna Doone – perhaps because he'd shown her the world inside books (even though in his own library, he'd blacked out the titles as 'a precaution against would-be borrowers'.) The diary becomes the stake between grandfather and grandmother: she finds it and threatens to show it to the bishop. That way she holds him to ransom, and he – well, he then has a cast-iron excuse to let things carry on the way they are. Even the most secret of documents speaks to someone to a purpose, Lorna knows, and autobiography – the wide range of what Dutch historians call 'Ego-documents' – fashions and re-fashions the self, in dialogue with imagined interlocutors, even if those imagined receivers are one's own future selves. The subjective 'I', the literary first person, has become a troubling ghost, there and not there, imagined or actual, dwelling in any number of texts, not least of *Bad Blood*; Lorna Sage writes here about one of Christine Brooke-Rose's novels, *Next*, in which the characters have stopped using the pronoun, I, because they own nothing, have no home, belong nowhere. You have to have all these coordinates to be a person who can speak for yourself.

Yet such a new emphasis on truth-telling sets a challenge to invention, to fabrication and to impersonation and performance, all the energies that leap in the fantastic, fairy tale and postmodern fictions that Lorna had so brilliantly interpreted and advocated. Lorna's argument gradually develops through the essays in *Moments of Truth*, that you can't have the work without the life or, more pointedly, the life without the work, nor the work or the life without the art. In other words, the grammar without the glamour. And she was going to pursue this theme in another book, to be called *Writing Lives*, to show that 'the "heroism" and representativeness of writers' life-stories [are] aspects of the decay of classic literary realism . . .'

The title Lorna chose for this collection of essays – *Moments of Truth* – interestingly shifts Woolf's epiphanic 'Moments of Being' away from the feeling-of-what-happens (the modernist enterprise) towards truth-telling, and the knowing-what-happened, in the sense of revelatory events that make a difference, that cause a shift to take place. Lorna returns again and again to a key concept in Beauvoir's thinking – the idea of *mauvaise foi*, or bad faith, which the French writer loathed, and diagnosed in bourgeois and clerical hypocrisy, in lyrical, confessional manifestations in writing, in short, in any public show of virtue, literary, social, religious and personal. I think there may be an echo of this phrase in the title of Lorna's memoir, but with a twist – because the phrase 'bad blood' both claims and rejects her inheritance, it revels in it as a badge of honour and at the same time relishes the irony that with all this family stuff behind her, she escaped, she stopped the stain – the so-called stain – seeping. She was a bad girl, perhaps, but she could also tell when something was in bad faith. In *Moments of Truth*, Lorna Sage has discerned a pattern in the way women writers of the last century made their exits from bargains involving bad faith – both on their part and on the part of others.

The book is a sequel to her *Women in the House of Fiction* (1992), but it engages more tenaciously with the issues of determinism in life and realism in literature, to probe the roughness and porousness of the female ego that texts are busy picking, unpicking, weaving, unweaving. The mesh that holds someone in social, economic and above all emotional obligations could be as sticky and strong as a pupa, if you like, but it could also be abruptly torn and cast aside. She traces these moments through the writings, quoting for example Christina Stead saying, 'another fatal idea that belongs to the bourgeoisie, that there's something sacred inside which if you dig out it will make you an original . . . There's nothing inside.' Of one of Jane Bowles's characters, Lorna comments, 'Miss Goering disinherits herself, in short, and becomes an adventuress, and a serious lady. That is, a woman who turns her true character into an open question.'

It is also surely relevant here that Lorna's own experience of time changed as her illness – asthma, emphysema – got a more and more unshakeable grip on her. She was looking back to see where she had come from, and it prompted her to inquire more closely into the play of light – and shade – from personal histories on Jean Rhys's way of looking at men, at Violet

Trefusis's comedy of manners in high places, on Djuna Barnes's eccentric bohemia. Her subjects emerge in all their singularity – her word – as people living in time and place, but in continuous conflictual dialogue with their given circumstances, as the young Lorna herself was, growing up in Hanmer on the Welsh borders. Was she attracted to fatality? Or does some terrible boozy, hacking nemesis keep coming after women writers? Lorna loathes sentiment and even romance; she doesn't focus on issues of self-destruction or premature demise, and she never reads the works backwards through their makers' deaths, because that would fall into the mythographers' sticky clutches.

Instead, through close individual studies of other people and their writing, Lorna gradually pieces together another way of telling the story of modern literature in which writers aren't acting in character, or bearing out behaviourists' and functional anthropologists' theories of nurture, but making themselves up as they go along: becoming new beings made of words, like one of Arcimboldo's allegories, creating their own 'profane interiorities'. As Lorna traces her subjects' features, the collection becomes a stimulating, original, idiosyncratic portrait gallery or private pantheon, almost in the manner of the baroque literature about amazons, angels, winged griffins and demons that was one of her first loves (one of her early essays was about Milton's *Comus*), when books were published with titles such as 'Galerie des femmes fortes' and Bess of Hardwick commissioned embroidered wall hangings of mythological and biblical heroines. She liked my own study of allegorical female figures, *Monuments & Maidens*, perhaps for this reason, that they represented a huge and mighty female host who could be marshalled to a new cause.

Recognising women of spirit also provided a guiding principle for *The Cambridge Guide to Women's Writing*, a huge undertaking that Lorna Sage edited single-handedly from 1992 to 1998.

Original, electric, witty (an unusual attribute of a reference work), it came out the year before *Bad Blood*; the two works, at opposite ends of the literary spectrum, embody Lorna's distinctive contribution to the debate about literature and gender. The *Guide* ranges far and wide over the globe, including all literatures in English from every epoch and in every genre, including traditionally relegated forms such as children's writings, fairy tales, romance, science fiction, slave memoirs, essays. Characteristically, it never bends the knee to pieties or precepts, from whatever source; Lorna's own style of criticism sets a pace for the contributors, close to the 'lightness' and 'quickness' and 'exactitude' singled out as literary qualities by Calvino in his *Six Memos for the Millennium*, published just after his death.

Heroism here lies in discovering a voice and speaking up: *Moments of Truth* listens in, filters out interference, picks up the individual resonance. Lorna herself continued to treat all problems of interpretation as open questions: doubt, scepticism, dissatisfaction keep her reading and her writing crackling with energy. It's characteristic that in her *London Review of Books* review of Jeremy Treglown's biography of Henry Green, the last piece Lorna wrote, you can hear her impatience with the reticence, even silence at the centre of Green's final compact with life: 'Asked for his opinions on the world, he'd tell people one should sit as still as possible, try not to go out. He didn't actually talk helpfully to interviewers ... he simply adopted a parody of the correct language.'[5] This stance could provide 'protective colouring' for survival, a stratagem Lorna Sage understood well from characters in Jean Rhys; but none of Lorna Sage's female subjects ever used it as a literary manoeuvre, or beat this kind of retreat – least of all herself.

There's a wonderful photograph, among many such in *Bad Blood*, showing Lorna at the Coronation Day Parade in 1953;

even dressed as Little Bo Peep, with beribboned crook and apron and scrip, her trimmed straw hat's subtly cocked and there's a defiant light in her eye (she will get into Arcadia, she will confront the Faerie Queene). Later, at the time I first met her, she put paid to all the typecasting sneer and scoffing commonly compacted then into the term 'female academic'; with her long slender transparent hands, her elegant feet, her blue eyes, her husky, torch singer voice, and her liking for being driven about in her husband Rupert Hodson's large squishy leather upholstered motor, she pioneered proof that you could be brilliant and learned and incisive – and blonde. The week she died, when I was asked to write a tribute for the *Independent* obituary page, I remembered meeting her by chance in Florence one time, and how she'd reminded me then of Beatrice, who, with her own luminous Botticelli tresses, guides the poet through the nine fixed spheres towards the stars while disquisitioning with occasional severity, and flashes of impatience, on everything from poetry to astronomy to theology as she does so.

Marina Warner
Kentish Town
May 2001

Notes

1. It was Angela Carter, I think, who first told me this odd scrap of etymological lore.
2. Angela Carter, *The Sadeian Woman* (1979), reprinted New York: Penguin, 2001.
3. 'Death of the Author', *Granta*, 1993, pp. 235–54, at p. 240.
4. Said in conversation with Frank Kermode and Marina Warner, at PEN, March 2001.
5. 'Landlocked', *London Review of Books*, 25 January 2001.

I

EDITH WHARTON

Ethan Frome

Edith Wharton always talked about *Ethan Frome* as the book in which she came into her own as a writer. She was nearly fifty when it was published in 1911, and had produced three long novels, three collections of stories, poems and a couple of other novellas, plus books on houses, gardens, travel. 'But', she wrote in her autobiography, *A Backward Glance*,

> the book to the making of which I brought the greatest joy and the fullest ease was '*Ethan Frome*'. For years I had wanted to draw life as it really was in the derelict mountain villages of New England, a life even in my time, and a thousandfold more a generation earlier, utterly unlike that seen through the rose-coloured spectacles of my predecessors, Mary Wilkins and Sarah Orme Jewett. In those days the snow-bound villages of Western Massachusetts were still grim places, morally and physically: insanity, incest and slow mental and moral starvation were hidden away behind the paintless wooden house-fronts of the long village street, or in the isolated farm-houses on the neighbouring hills . . .

This was not supposed to be her territory at all. The world in which she had grown up and married was urban, wealthy, 'social' to a fault ('old' New York), and more recently – since

3

1907 – she had become increasingly an expatriate, settled in Paris. Her most successful novel to date, *The House of Mirth* (1905), had dealt with the world she knew – cluttered with conventions, riven with luxurious scruples. Yet it was to *Ethan Frome*'s bleak, wintry landscape that she brought 'fullest ease'.

For she saw herself as a realist ('I had wanted to draw life as it really was'). Although she protested more than once that the poor were no more real than the rich – 'the assumption that the people I write about are not "real" because they are not navvies and charwomen, makes me feel rather hopeless' – she had inherited from such nineteenth-century European novelists as George Eliot the idea that realistic fiction had a duty to embrace and meld whole worlds of difference. Wharton never quite managed this, or even seriously tried to, inside the covers of one book (though a working girl puts in a problematic and providential appearance in the last scenes of *The House of Mirth*, for instance), but in *Ethan* she did escape from her caste into another, almost into otherness itself. This must partly explain why she felt such exhilaration in the writing: if the theme was grinding poverty, the experience of crossing over was a joy.

It was a world that reminded her of *Wuthering Heights* – 'Emily Brontë would have found as savage tragedies in our remoter valleys as on her Yorkshire moors' (*A Backward Glance*). And when she chose names for her main characters she went to another 'savage' source, Nathaniel Hawthorne, though as Sandra Gilbert and Susan Gubar point out, Wharton's character Zenobia, the ailing, older wife, the clog that keeps her hero tied down, is 'strikingly different from Hawthorne's proud and beautiful heroine . . . for Wharton the glamorous and threatening strength of Hawthorne's Zenobia was . . . unrealistic' (*War of the Words*). She was making her own way, in short, and the signs of that were her measures of distance from her American

4

predecessors – and in particular the one predecessor critics had already decided was her main mentor, Henry James. In striking out into this harsh, rural region Wharton was turning for the moment away from her friend James, too. He belonged to the civilised, cosmopolitan, overfurnished spaces.

In fact, she complained of James that his late work was 'more and more lacking in atmosphere, more and more severed from that thick nourishing human air in which we all live and move' (*A Backward Glance*). She was after something cruder and more provincial than his example offered and whether or not it is a matter of 'influence' at all (I suspect not), her closest affinities in *Ethan Frome* are with a novelist at the opposite end of the late nineteenth-century spectrum, Thomas Hardy – like herself an heir to George Eliot, and also like her in pursuing a belated, disillusioned realism. She did meet Hardy on occasion (she met everyone, very nearly), and found him 'as remote and incommunicative as our most unsocial American men of letters' (*A Backward Glance*), which may have been, for her purposes, exactly right. He was not at all cultivated in the James sense, but self-taught, an autodidact, an outsider – and for all her sophistication, that was what Wharton, like every other woman writer of her time, was too.

As a result the great intellectual movements of the later nineteenth century were not filtered or distanced for her by prior immersion in the Greek and Latin classics, or mediated by a university. Like Hardy, she dated her mental coming-of-age from understanding Darwin –

the great evolutionary movement . . . the first overwhelming sense of cosmic vastnesses which such 'magic case-ments' let into our little geocentric universe . . .

Through 'Darwin, Spencer and Lecky', whom she described as the greatest formative influences of her youth (*Letters*), she had been introduced to a sense of cosmic irony, a world in which – if you took the long view – you could see whole sub-species headed for extinction, and the struggle for survival petering out in sterile backwaters. This was very much Hardy's territory, particularly in *Jude the Obscure*. Ethan Frome is an American Jude. If his tragedy is less cruelly drawn-out it is, against the background of the *new* world, no less shocking. For Wharton, as for Hardy, being a realist often meant being what people would label a pessimist, seeing a ghastly neatness, a bleak irony beyond tragedy, in her characters' fates.

She was going back to her *intellectual* awakening in *Ethan Frome*, then, much more nakedly than before, and she gives Ethan himself a glimpse of the same cold cosmic spaces. Once upon a time he had fallen in love with his wife's cousin and live-in helper Mattie, partly because he could share his world-picture with her:

> ... at his side, living under his roof and eating his bread, was a creature to whom he could say: 'That's Orion down yonder; the big fellow to the right is Aldebaran, and the bunch of little ones – like bees swarming – they're the Pleiades ...' or whom he could hold entranced before a ledge of granite thrusting up through the fern while he unrolled the huge panorama of the ice age, and the long dim stretches of succeeding time.

Ethan's community is blighted, decaying, dying very, very slowly. As he says to the narrator,

> We're kinder side-tracked here now ... I've always set

6

down the worst of mother's trouble to that . . . After the trains begun running nobody ever come by here to speak of, and mother never could get it through her head what had happened, and it preyed on her right along till she died.

He himself, horribly maimed now, old before his time, endures a living death while he waits to join the rest of the Fromes in the graveyard. Unlike his mother he sees very well what is happening, but he cannot escape it. He is the last of his line.

Edith Wharton got to know the kind of dead-alive New England hamlets she is describing by taking excursions in her chauffeur-driven motor car. If the railway was the characteristic nineteenth-century sign of progress and of the dynamism of industrial 'evolution', then the automobile became its twentieth-century counterpart – representing a new style of mobility, freedom and independence. Remote places lay open to inspection:

> there was inexhaustible delight in penetrating to the remoter parts of Massachusetts and New Hampshire, discovering derelict villages with Georgian churches and balustraded house-fronts . . . My two New England tales, 'Ethan Frome' and 'Summer', were the result of explorations among villages still bedrowsed in a decaying rural existence, and sad slow-speaking people living in conditions hardly changed since their forebears held those villages against the Indians. (*A Backward Glance*)

One should dwell a little on this image of Wharton touring the territory of her tragedy – a woman of enormous energy, wealth and creative curiosity finding her subject in the 'insanity, incest and slow mental and moral starvation' of the near-extinct inhabitants she observed on her travels. The contrast between Wharton and her subject could not be more striking.

However, the tale's most strange and powerful effect is one of *recognition*. For all the fascination with the otherness of Ethan's life, the true shudder comes at the moment when Wharton's intrusive narrator steps over the threshold into the farmhouse kitchen, and the reader is taken into the inside story of Ethan, Zeena and Mattie, into the past and into a place that is, somehow, intimately familiar. This is the other major ingredient in Wharton's exhilaration over the writing of *Ethan Frome*. She had found a setting that embodied her most private creative space, 'that mysterious fourth-dimensional world which is the artist's inmost sanctuary and on the *threshold* of which enquiry must perforce halt' (my italics), as she described it in *The Writing of Fiction*.

In another place she says that 'each time the artist passes from dream to execution he will need to find the rules and formulas *on the threshold*' (*The Writing of Fiction*, my italics). This image of the threshold symbolises for her an escape into the 'fourth-dimensional' world of art, and to understand its power one needs to look at the way she saw her vocation. In her autobiography she remembers her reaction to the publication of her first stories, *The Greater Inclination* (1899): 'thereafter I never questioned that story-telling was my job . . . I felt like some homeless waif who after trying for years to take out naturalisation papers and being rejected by every country, has finally acquired a nationality. The Land of Letters was henceforth to be my country . . .' Wharton found herself in the mirror of the fiction. She became mentally independent of the ladylike world she grew up in ('story-telling was *my job*'). She had felt increasingly that her sexual and domestic life was a prison; now she built a 'sanctuary' inside it.

Ethan's life-in-death was utterly familiar to her. In *The House of Mirth* she had explored the decay of old New York society in the face of the invasion by new money and new values and, though her class suffered from poverty of imagination and lack of vitality, not her hero's literal deprivation, she recognised the same inertia at work in their rule-bound lives. Another of her early novels, much less well-known, *The Fruit of the Tree* (1907), shows her working out at greater length, and rather falteringly, the central elements of the *Ethan* story. The dreadful sledding 'accident' in which Ethan and Mattie made their bid for death and freedom but which they have so horribly survived to live on together with Ethan's invalid wife Zeena in that claustrophobic kitchen is anticipated in *The Fruit of the Tree* — where Wharton uses 'coasting' downhill on a sledge as an image of loss-of-self, of bliss, of unanimity and innocence:

> . . . the spell of the long white slope, and the tingle of cold in her veins. 'Shall we go down? Should you like it?'
> . . . his whole body burned with a strange intensity of life . . . the level sun dazzled their eyes, and the first plunge seemed to dash them down into darkness . . . They had dropped below the sunset and were tearing through the clear nether twilight of the descent . . . It seemed to Amherst as though his body had been left behind, and only the spirit in him rode the wild blue currents of galloping air.

Later in the story the woman is horribly injured and lingers on in 'useless pain'. 'I wish to God she had been killed', says her father. Her nurse in fact mercifully helps her die with morphine then marries her widowed husband.

The *Ethan* plot elements are scrambled in this earlier version

– the bid for orgasmic release, the nightmare of a kind of life after death in lingering paralysis, the blasphemous but brave thought that there are worse things than dying. (In *Ethan* it is the narrator's landlady who says it: 'they all thought Mattie couldn't live. Well, I say it's a pity she *did*.') Mobility, escape, the 'spell' of the irreversible flight are protests against mere existence. In *Ethan* they are turned back on themselves. What Wharton really wants to say is that taking euphoric flight somehow *necessarily* leads to this higher vision of unfreedom that she calls realism.

The very form of the story spells out the message. Ethan, when the narrator meets him, has long been maimed and defeated, and the 'frame' tale which takes us to the kitchen threshold, and into the flashback that recaptures Ethan's and Mattie's abortive suicide attempt, effectively exiles all their vivid anguish to the past. Thus the end was implicit in the beginning, though Wharton saves the portrait of Mattie as a whining cripple for the *bitter* end. This is exactly the sort of closed fictional structure that she says is nearest to her heart –

> It is always a necessity to me that the note of inevitableness should be sounded at the very opening of my tale, and that my characters should go forward to their ineluctable doom like the 'murdered man' in 'The Pot of Basil'. From the first I know exactly what is going to happen to every one of them; their fate is settled beyond rescue, and I have but to watch and record. (*A Backward Glance*)

Wharton's sense of power and freedom as an artist is wedded to a vision of life frustrated. She takes ironic satisfaction in identifying with representatives of dying breeds, 'side-tracked' in the evolutionary game. Novelist Cynthia Ozick, who disapproves of many things about Wharton, nonetheless puts her finger on the right pulse when she writes that there is 'outside the writing – no destination' ('Justice (Again) to Edith Wharton', *What Henry James Knew*).

Wharton's own private life was also in crisis around this time – she was deciding at long last to divorce her sad, unstable husband Teddy; and she was involved in the one passionate love-affair of her life, with journalist Morton Fullerton. 'You woke me from a long lethargy, a dull acquiescence in conventional restrictions, a needless self-effacement,' she had written to Fullerton in 1908. But as it turned out he had woken her to a passion that had no future, except perhaps in her work and her heightened sensitivity to pain. She did divorce Teddy, but she never saw divorce as a key to real freedom; in this, too, she identified with the old, dying order. In a much later novel, *The Mother's Recompense* (1925), she shows how determinedly she saw the new freedoms as a version of the old constrictions. Here a wife makes her escape from a stifling marriage, leaving her baby daughter behind, and falls in love with a much younger man. Their affair peters out, sadly, but life wreaks its revenge on her when after her ex-husband's death she is reunited with her long-lost daughter only to find that her daughter is, by a dreadful coincidence, in love with her ex-lover. The melodramatic savagery of this contrived plot serves to underline Wharton's conviction that you cannot escape from the past. Once again, in this rather bad novel, the tell-tale imagery of *Ethan* springs to life. When the heroine returns to her ex-husband's house we are told: 'She had dreamed of the hated threshold and yearned for it.' When she flies from the house, down the stairs for the second time, running away from the 'incestuous' spectacle of her daughter in the arms of her ex-lover, the repetition is unbearable:

11

Her precipitate descent recalled the early winter morning when, as hastily, almost as unconsciously, she had descended those same stairs, flying from her husband's house. Nothing was changed in the hall.

As she had earlier realised:

> It was all, in short, as natural and unnatural, as horrible, intolerable and inescapable, as if she had become young again, with all her desolate and unavoidable life stretching away ahead of her to – this.

The Mother's Recompense reveals the persistence of Wharton's obsession with the image of the *impasse*, the dead-end, the irony of going on living after it is clear there is no future – 'The bitterness of death was passed, yes – but the bitterness of what came after?'

Sometimes she did allow herself to imagine a way out, though. In the novella *Summer* (1916), for example, her young heroine Charity is seduced and abandoned by a lover, and marries her adoptive 'father' in a characteristically incestuous situation. Yet the feel of the tale is altogether more hopeful – Charity is pregnant by her lover, there will be new blood, a next generation, and this makes the defeat of her personal ambitions more bearable. *Ethan Frome*, however, offers no way out, it has a kind of perverse perfection in despair. The satisfactions it embodies are all writerly, a matter of art and of craft. It started life several years earlier, according to her autobiography, as a story in French written in order to improve her grasp of the language once she had decided to live in Paris. When she took it up again in English it seemed almost ready-formed to her pen.

I am driving harder and harder at that ridiculous novella [she wrote in January 1911], which has grown into a large, long-legged hobbledehoy of a young novel. 20,000 long it is already, and growing. I have to let its frocks down every day, and soon it will be in trousers! However, I see an end, for I'm over the hard explanatory part, and the *vitesse acquise* is beginning to rush me along . . . (*Letters*)

This ecstasy of writing was her sledge-ride, her consummation, her way of finding freedom in necessity.

The Custom of the Country

When she published *The Custom of the Country* in 1913, Edith Wharton was in her prime as a writer. She was fifty-one years old, she had been living in Paris for six years, *The House of Mirth* in 1905 and her writings since then had won her both commercial and critical success, and in 1911 she had sold her American house, and separated from her husband Teddy. Her divorce came through in 1913 too – a fact of some relevance to *The Custom of the Country*, which uses divorce as a plot device with the same prominence as novels of an earlier age had used marriage (or adultery). On the face of it, however, this is *not* a personal book, but one in which Wharton prides herself on her ability to look at her native land like a 'sociologist' (a new word she picks up and uses in its pages) and, rather less objectively, as a satirist. She is celebrating her exile by shining a cruelly revealing light on what she left behind: she calls her heroine Undine Spragg for a variety of humorous and mischievous reasons – it is a name that always makes readers wince, and is meant to – but it is obviously significant that Undine's initials match those of the United States.

We also know some of the questions the title of the novel was meant to raise, since Wharton invents a character called Charles Bowen, a middle-aged and patrician American observer of the fashionable scene, whose main task is to hold forth on the topic:

> ... the average American looks down on his wife ...
> How much does he let her share in the real business
> of life? How much does he rely on her judgement and
> help in the conduct of serious affairs? ... it's against the
> custom of the country ... the European woman ... [is] not
> a parenthesis, as she is here – she's in the very middle of the
> picture ... Where does the real life of most American men
> lie? In some woman's drawing-room or in their offices?

Bowen, who belongs (as did Wharton) to 'old' New York, a
world of inherited wealth and puritan manners, prefers European
customs (even if they are somewhat 'effete') to the new style of
capitalist America. The new rich separate out the spheres of men
and women more radically than ever before: on the one hand,
women are trivialised by being exiled from the action, having
nothing to do with Wall Street, and the economic battlefield; on
the other, the money-men have neither the leisure nor the liberal
education to belong to a *salon*. The common ground between
the sexes, therefore, is getting smaller, and the institution that
symbolises sharing – marriage – is beginning to fall to pieces.
After World War I, in 1919, Wharton published a book of essays
entitled *French Ways and their Meanings*, in which she returned
to the issue. French women had less legal independence, she
argued, but in practice they exercised much more real power.
An American woman when she marries 'is cut off from men's
society in all but the most formal and intermittent ways. On her
wedding day she ceases ... to be an influence in the lives of
the men of the community to which she belongs.' All of which
makes it sound easy to establish where Wharton stands: for the
old, against the new. But, of course, it is not so simple.

Her own career as a writer had distanced her from the values
of her family, and of people like her character Charles Bowen,

who are content merely to *observe*. In her autobiography *A Backward Glance*, she looked back with great feeling to her first published volume of stories in 1899 – 'thereafter I never questioned that story-telling was my job,' she wrote, and her choice of words was, as always, significant. To call writing a 'job' was to make it real, commercial, practical – not romantic, otherworldly, ladylike. In short, she grew up with money, but it was the money she earned that gave her self-respect. And in *The Custom of the Country*, we are never allowed to forget the value of energy and ingenuity and resilience, all qualities she had in abundance. Edith Wharton the writer was herself an example of untraditional enterprise. She had become, as she said, a citizen of the Land of Letters, and so could stay imaginatively independent of the customs of both countries.

Her heroine Undine's adventures certainly take Wharton into uncharted territory as far as the conventions of novelistic plotting are concerned. To begin with, we assume that we are reading the story of a young lady's entrance into the world – the time-honoured formula that was first given classic embodiment in Fanny Burney's *Evelina* in 1778. However, it is soon clear that the expected drama of social initiation is complicated by the fact that back in her native city of Apex, Undine, young as she is, has a 'past' which she and her parents are anxious to cover up, involving the vulgar but go-getting Elmer Moffatt. According to convention, this ought to mean that she has been seduced and betrayed, or at the very least her reputation has been besmirched by scandal, but in fact, as we learn belatedly and by teasing inches, Undine and Elmer have been married *and divorced* – a sort of instant shot-gun divorce engineered by Mr Spragg on economic and social grounds, with Undine's full co-operation. If she seems curiously fresh, untouched, virginal, it is because in the essential sense – essential to Undine and the new breed of woman she represents – of *social* identity her experience has left her unchanged. She is still, in other words, as eagerly upwardly mobile as ever, as ready to begin on the world. Far from being the plot's central event and grand destination, then, marriage is already (in Wall Street language) 'discounted' long before Undine marries the civilised and sensitive only son of distinguished 'old' money – and not much of that – Ralph Marvell. Once again, we may expect her, when discontent stirs, to commit adultery in grand, tragic nineteenth-century-novel fashion, but no: she divorces Ralph, and starts on the world again . . . Divorce becomes, in the context of Wharton's black-comic exaggeration, synonymous with Americanness. Thus, the Princess Estradina, explaining Undine's temporary lack of a husband, says, 'But she's an American – she's divorced . . .' as if she were merely stating the same fact in different ways. Undine becomes the stuff of which gossip columns are made, the figurehead of the new century's love-affair with beauty, wealth, fashion *and publicity*, as modern as a motor car and much more expensive.

She is the ideal consumer because she is so restless: in an older kind of plot, when new money met property they settled down together and stood for continuity – change, yes, but change rooted in tradition. Undine is all energy, for her changefulness has become the order of things, she is a kind of mutant who lives on noise, bright lights and a supply of strangers. She likes to live in hotels, and contrives to make her private sitting-rooms and boudoirs look like hotel suites, all mirrors and gilt chairs and 'decor'. Wharton gets a good deal of fun out of Undine's vulgarity, and the banality of her taste. Even when she learns refinement (and she learns all the time) she never succeeds in settling into her own style; she is always anxiously on the look-out for a newer way to be.

This is more than a superior authorial joke about the gaffes of social climbers, however. Undine is the latest incarnation of the frontier spirit. Her maternal grandfather (as Ralph Marvell learns from Mrs Spragg) was an inventor:

'Why, we called her after a hair-waver father put on the market the week she was born . . .' It's from *un*doolay, you know, the French for crimping; father always thought the name made it take . . . No, father didn't start *in* as a druggist,' she went on, expanding with the signs of Marvell's interest; 'he was educated for an undertaker, and built up a first-class business; but he was always a beautiful speaker, and after a while he sorter drifted into the ministry. Of course it didn't pay anything like as well, so finally he opened a drug-store, and he did first-rate at that too, though his heart was always in the pulpit. But after he made such a success with his hair-waver he got speculating in land . . .'

Undine's grandfather sounds like a parodic version of the kind of hero of self-improvement Samuel Smiles eulogised in his enterprise bible *Self-Help* (1859). Yet there is a serious point lurking behind this carnival of opportunism, an idea about adaptability. Edith Wharton, as she said in her autobiography, was much influenced by Darwin on evolution (*The Origin of Species* was published the same year as *Self-Help*), and whenever she imagines change Darwinian models creep in. Undine's grandfather, her father, and the various other new people who hail from towns like Apex and flourish on Wall Street, have an impressive capacity for reinventing *themselves* to suit the climate of speculation. Elmer Moffatt in particular (Mr Spragg misjudged him) proves brilliantly resourceful –

'something in his look seemed to promise the capacity to develop into any character he might care to assume'. 'I'm carrying a whole new line of goods,' he tells Spragg. While Ralph Marvell contemplates 'the drama of "business"' in distancing quotation marks, and only looks on at 'the fierce interplay of its forces', he recognises that Moffatt comes alive on that battlefield: 'He strikes me as the kind of man who develops slowly, needs a big field, and perhaps makes some big mistakes, but gets where he wants to in the end . . . There's something epic about him – a kind of epic effrontery.' Undine is the female of *this* species ('animated by her father's business instinct') and there is something epic about her too.

Named by her creator, if not her parents, after a water-nymph, Undine is related to the nereids, classical sea-nymphs with a suggestion of the siren, who are sometimes portrayed like mermaids, with fishes' tails. Her beauty is described as both statuesque and sinuous:

> She was always doubling and twisting on herself, and every movement she made seemed to start at the nape of her neck, just below the lifted roll of reddish-gold hair, and flow without a break through her whole slim length to the tips of her fingers and the points of her slender restless feet.

If, as seems likely, Wharton is playing with the idea that Undine represents a new, mutant, development of (female) human nature, then the fishiness is appropriate, since it is an evolution that is also in many ways a simplification, a return of the primitive. Morally, Undine is certainly fishy, as Ralph reflects – 'She would go on eluding and doubling . . . and at that game she was sure to beat him in the end'. Ralph, who thought of a fine phrase from Montaigne – *diverse et ondoyante* – to describe

19

her at the beginning, before his disillusion, belongs by contrast to a human sub-species so refined, specialised and incapable of radical change that his family seem, even to him, 'doomed to extinction', soon to be 'exhibited at ethnological shows', while he himself is a gentleman of the traditional type, with a 'passive openness to the finer sensations'. We are told that it had long been clear to Charles Bowen 'that poor Ralph was a survival, and destined, as such, to go down in any conflict with the rising forces'. Ralph's discovery that the Undine he poetically imagined and married is a romantic fiction drives him to a breakdown and (eventually, when Undine threatens to take their son) suicide: his strength of feeling is, in the survival stakes, a handicap.

The marriage market has its ups and downs, and Undine too faces defeat at moments:

> Not much more than a year had elapsed since Undine . . . had heard the immense orchestral murmur of Paris rise through the open windows like the ascending movement of her own hopes. The immense murmur still sounded on, deafening and implacable as some elemental force; and the discord in her fate no more disturbed it than the motor wheels rolling by under the windows were disturbed by the particles of dust that they ground to finer powder as they passed.

Instead of succumbing to this intimation of the world's indifference, however, she goes off to bide her time in a Riviera hotel, where she meets the Princess Estradina, and is able to step back on to the great stage. This eloquent passage on the sound of the city's traffic is deliberately designed by Wharton to match Ralph's ecstatic sense of oneness with nature on their honeymoon – 'On the blackness of cork and ilex and cypress lay the green and purple lustres . . . of old bronze . . . night after night the skies were wine-blue and bubbling with stars . . . such mergings of the personal with the general life that one felt oneself a mere wave on the wild stream of being.' Ralph's readiness to merge with nature around him points to one of the novel's paradoxes: that he is a much more *feminine* figure than Undine. He may see himself as a poet, Undine as his Muse, but his secret language of vocation is all about a 'cave' inside his psyche – 'a secret inaccessible place with glaucous lights, mysterious murmurs . . .' – which makes him sound pregnant with his vocation. (He does turn out to be a much better parent to their child than Undine, of course.)

Because Ralph is a would-be artist, and a scion of old New York, critics have wanted, naturally enough, to find in him a figure for Wharton herself. Candace Waid in particular, in *Edith Wharton's Letters from the Underworld: Fictions of Women and Writing* (1991), reads *The Custom of the Country* as 'about the destruction of the writer who is seduced by the siren song of a false muse'. But while Wharton undoubtedly likes Ralph, and pities him dreadfully, he is surely not *her* kind of artist – he is altogether too lyrical, too passive, too humourless to stand for her. And, of course, he doesn't actually get around to writing, or publishing. His reason is that he has to slave away in an office to support Undine, but this very separation of art and work is one Wharton denied – 'I never questioned that story-telling was *my job*.' Only once or twice in the course of his self-communings on art does Ralph sound much like his creator – once when he thinks that his projected book will have to be 'what the masterpieces of literature had mostly been – a pot-boiler', and once much later, when he is trying to accommodate his disillusion:

The vision that had come to him had no likeness to any of

his earlier imaginings. Two or three subjects had haunted him . . . but these now seemed either too lyrical or too tragic. He no longer saw life on the heroic scale: he wanted to do something in which men should look no bigger than the insects they were . . .

This time he gets further than ever before, with a draft chapter – but he hasn't Wharton's stomach for irony and black comedy, and dies of despair and disgust.

Wharton is horribly amused by the spectacle of Undine's and Elmer's progress, and in a way she admires their resilience and their industry ('I've got my job,' says Elmer, even when he is far too rich to need to work). In her Parisian exile she can contemplate the monstrous alliance of Wall Street and Fifth Avenue with a kind of fascinated lucidity, for she herself also belongs to the modern world, one of the *Women of the Left Bank* Shari Benstock writes about, along with Gertrude Stein or Nathalie Barney. As Benstock says, they lived in very different styles; Wharton didn't 'know' such Bohemian contemporaries (though she did know Proust's friend Anna de Nouailles), but their very juxtaposition gives food for thought. Wharton was not a literary *modernist*; her techniques hark back to nineteenth-century realism and the world of (say) George Eliot, whom she is almost paraphrasing in that line about 'mergings of the personal life with the general life' (itself an intuition Eliot inherited from Romantic poets, Wordsworth in particular). But like her older English contemporary Thomas Hardy, Wharton sees that the post-Darwinian world of the survival of the fittest won't sustain a realist reading – you tip over into black comedy and irony and a bleak vision of dwarfed aspirations.

Ways of life you thought were rooted in nature turn out to have been a mere phase in a larger development, so that the old 'real' itself starts to look quaint and false and superseded. As a much later American novelist, Mary McCarthy, put it – 'the novel, with its common sense, is of all forms the least adapted to encompass the modern world, whose leading characteristic is irreality'. She means of course the *realist* novel:

> The novel, after all, is the literary form dedicated to the representation of our common world, i.e., not merely the common ordinary world, but the world we have in common ... Common sense, also known as the reality principle, rules the novel ...
>
> (*Occasional Prose*)

It is precisely the absence of common ground between Undine and Ralph that Wharton focuses on. One of the book's great cruel, comic moments is when, on the honeymoon, Undine reveals that she has simply loathed the whole trip, and found his version of Europe – Italian cities, little hill towns, churches and olive groves – smelly, hot and unintelligible: 'All these places seem as if they were dead. It's all like some awful cemetery.' He realises too that she is 'sick to death of being alone with him'. The allusions to death are suggestive – what he reads as the signs of tradition and continuity and intimacy of connection she feels as traps and ties and hindrances to her freedom, denying her right to *life*.

And life for her starts in self-love and the image framed in the mirror. *Her* secret place is not somewhere inside, but outside, on the hard surface of the looking-glass:

> ... Undine bolted her door, dragged the tall pier-glass forward and, rummaging in a drawer for fan and gloves, swept to a seat before the mirror with the air of a lady

arriving at an evening party . . . the white and gold room, with its blazing wall-brackets, formed a sufficiently brilliant background . . . So untempered a glare would have been destructive to all half-tones and subtleties of modelling; but Undine's beauty was as vivid, and almost as crude, as the brightness suffusing it. Her black brows, her reddish-tawny hair and the pure red and white of her complexion defied the searching decomposing radiance: she might have been some fabled creature whose home was in a beam of light.

She might, in fact, have been a film star (truly at home in a beam of light) if the cinema had at the time been advanced enough for Wharton to use it for the comparison. Undine is in Technicolor, she lives and breathes in what McCarthy calls 'irreality', in radiant emotional isolation. In a box at the opera (on the social stage herself) she experiences an agony of vitality:

> Undine felt that quickening of the faculties that comes in the high moments of life. Her consciousness seemed to take in at once the whole bright curve of the auditorium, from the unbroken lines of spectators below her to the culminating blaze of the central chandelier; and she herself was the core of that vast illumination, the sentient throbbing surface which gathered all the shafts of light into a centre.

She loves to be desired, but feels no physical wants on her own account: she is 'remote and Ariel-like', possessed of 'the coolness of the element from which she took her name'. A crowded restaurant or ballroom, any public place, is for her alive with sex – 'the close contact of covetous impulses' – and we are told that her third husband, Raymond de Chelles, attractive as he is, is really only a kind of accessory: 'pushing at his side through blazing theatre-lobbies answered to her inmost ideal of domestic intimacy'. In the end, she kills the desires of the men who love her (both Ralph and Raymond turn away from her at night, after she has enjoyed a public orgy of admiration). Her frigidity seems to act as a pretty efficient contraceptive, too. The once she does conceive, she is appalled and resentful, diagnosing her condition with 'cold competence' and seeing the pregnancy through as a 'hateful compulsory exercise' that takes her out of circulation. Wharton characterises her consistently and rather frighteningly as someone with no insides, no inner life, no 'soul'. Left alone in a room she communes with the mirror, 'her only notion of self-seeing' is the 'image of herself in other minds'.

So in a sense (though she has secrets and tells lies) Undine has no private life. Doublings and reflections of herself are where she acquires a sort of *trompe-l'oeil* depth. She is, Wharton wants to say, the archetypal product of 'the custom of the country' which idealises self-invention and speculation. Oddly enough, although self-appointed 'sociologist' Charles Bowen is right that men and women seem separated off from each other in the new dispensation, one business ethic runs through both public and (supposedly) private life. As we have seen, Undine's intimate life *is* public (quite early on in her career she hires a press agent). If we modify Bowen's view to take this into account, then what we have is a vision of lives running along parallel lines, no converging, no 'merging' (in poor Ralph's vocabulary), no common cultural territory:

Every Wall Street term had its equivalent in the language of Fifth Avenue, and while he talked of building up railways she was building up palaces, and picturing all the multiple lives he would lead in them. To have things had always seemed to her the first essential of existence, and as she listened to him the vision of the things he could have unrolled itself before her like the long triumph of an Asiatic conqueror.

This grand mock-epic passage reveals Elmer and Undine as, after all, made for each other. The book's best feat of comic plotting is to keep their (non-)relationship always alive in the background. We are shown something of his ups and downs on the stock market, and a lot more of hers on the marriage market, as though they are quite unrelated strands, but in fact their lives are uncannily alike in their remorseless linearity, always discarding the past and looking to the future.

When they conspire at the start to erase the memory of their marriage back in Apex, and vow to help each other on, the language of their deal is a parody of the wedding-service. He promises to keep quiet, to enable her marriage into the Marvell family to go ahead, and exacts a promise in return:

> '. . . if ever it should come handy to know any of 'em in a business way, would you fix it up for me – *after you're married*?'
>
> Their eyes met, and she remained silent for a tremulous moment or two; then she held out her hand. 'Afterward – yes. I promise. And *you* promise, Elmer?'
>
> 'Oh, to have and to hold!' he sang out . . .

They are true to each other in being honest about their dishonesty. And *The Custom of the Country* can, as a result, stage a splendid parody of the conventional happy ending when they re-marry at last – now that Elmer is a millionaire. He has become, also, an obsessive collector (Persian rugs, paintings, jewels, tapestries), and it is in that spirit that he wants Undine. That she has belonged to other men in the interval bothers him not at all, any more than he minds that the Boucher tapestries that adorn their new house were heirlooms belonging to her French ex-husband's family. Rather, their value is enhanced.

Divorce is the (anti-)institution, the 'custom', which enables private life to adjust to the pressures of the market, and divorce is the 'fairy-tale' solution to the plot, in Wharton's comic world-turned-upside-down. Divorce symbolises the new style of speculation in flesh. One thing all Wharton's new-model Americans are agreed on is that sex outside marriage is a very bad idea, and unlikely to pay off. They despise the time-honoured complexity and decadence of Europe, where marriage is about patrilineal family obligations, and meshed in a complex surrounding network of lovers and friends, the setting for tragedy (or high comedy). The new divorcees are deeply puritan, the notion of sex for pleasure disgusts them, and sex for procreation isn't much better. Elmer shows that he is indeed worthy of Undine by standing out for marriage, when she – married to a Catholic, and seemingly trapped – offers him an adulterous liaison. He wants to own her in public, to parade her as a possession, he has no interest in clandestine pleasure, for he rightly sees that intimacy is not her gift nor her point. Only in public is she an object of desire, so he grandly offers her his millions in order to obtain the book's most prized sign of respect – a divorce.

While she was writing *The Custom of the Country*, which was begun in 1908, Edith Wharton had enjoyed (and suffered) a secret love-affair with American journalist Morton Fullerton, and had convinced herself of the value of their passion, even though it led nowhere: 'You woke me from a long lethargy,' she wrote to him. Undine is never awoken sensuously, hence her indignant conviction of her own innocence. Physical intimacy has no psychic dimension for her, she would never understand why Ralph is tipped over the edge into suicide by the discovery that before she met him she had been married to Elmer (or rather, as Elmer puts it, 'I've been divorced from her myself'). In Ralph this conjures up the most appalling 'nausea', a grotesque sense of physical closeness to Elmer, as if the two of *them* had made love. He finds himself oppressed by the other man's bodily presence – 'the growth of short black hair on his manicured hands, even the tiny cracks and crow's-feet . . .'

This terrible (and horribly funny) revelation points to one of Wharton's most prescient intuitions – that the apparently dominant position of the Undines of the American world is deceptive. The power stays with their spouses, they are messages exchanged by the (new) men. This was a point Simone de Beauvoir made years later, commenting on the myth of the 'castrating' American woman – 'even if it is true that the spirit of revenge in her has been exasperated to the point of making her a "praying mantis", she still remains a dependent and relative being; America is a masculine world' (*The Prime of Life*). And this is yet another facet of Undine's looking-glass identity – that she operates for others, *and for herself*, as a symbol. She symbolises American freedom, enterprise, energy, but she only 'has' these things in a problematic, rather unconvincing sense. Marina Warner's reading of the symbolic message of a much more famous American icon of the later nineteenth century, the Statue of Liberty, makes some pertinent points. The sculptor Bartholdi, she observes, 'shifted the allusion of Liberty away from unbridled Nature in favour of an imagery of control and light' (*Monuments and Maidens*), and again, 'Liberty is not representing her own freedom'.

Edith Wharton put her finger on one of the most significant

cultural changes of her time – one we are still coming to terms with: the importance of communications, the penetration of roads, railways (Elmer is a railway millionaire), newspaper headlines, telegrams, telephones into almost all corners of our world. Undine reads about the life she wants in the newspapers when she is a girl in Apex, and she achieves it – levitates into the pages she used to read, as a headline heroine. The media (you could say) no longer simply 'report' or come after events, they are a major force in events. It is this 'irreality' that Wharton addresses in the novel – which is perhaps why the main bearer of continuity is the squat comic figure of Mrs Heeny, the society masseuse with a fat black bag full of press-clippings. She is there in the first scene, and at the end it is her clippings that Undine's son Paul consults to find out what his mother has been up to, and who his father is now. Mrs Heeny's reading from her sacred texts sets the black comic seal on the action – 'No case has ever been railroaded through the divorce courts . . . at a higher rate of speed . . . every record has been broken.' Mrs Heeny is the oracle of a coming age when indeed the records will all be broken, and the past will only be recoverable in splintered shards. An exaggeration for the purposes of comedy, of course – and Wharton prided herself on having the prescience and tough-mindedness to laugh rather than despair.

II

VIRGINIA WOOLF

The Voyage Out

Virginia Woolf hit upon the title of her first novel quite casually, on a trip to Portugal with her younger brother Adrian in 1905: 'we discovered on the voyage out that we ought to have booked passage on the return boat'.[1] As far as we know, it was about three years before she started the book, and another three after that (1911) before she fished up the phrase and called it *The Voyage Out*. In fact she had put a name to one of the archetypal subtexts of first novels. The novel of beginning on the world is a rite of passage, an odyssey of sorts. It is where you 'find your bearings' as a writer. Woolf's Portuguese excursion was her only real sea voyage, but the metaphor of taking ship and watching the solid land drift away was the compelling thing. She wanted to shrink England and get English life into a new perspective. The novel is full of passages that glory in the queasy shifts of viewpoint you can engineer by first going to sea. In 1908, when she was working on an early draft in Manorbier in South Wales, she wrote to Clive Bell in euphoric mood: 'Ah, it is the sea that does it! perpetual movement, and a border of mystery, solving the limits of fields, and silencing their prose.'[2] When Rachel Vinrace boards her father's cargo boat bound for South America, she is embarking on a course from which there is no turning back.

The writing took a long time: Woolf rewrote and revised repeatedly, and fell ill again and again in the process. After correcting the proofs in 1913 she attempted suicide, not for the first time, and the book didn't finally come out until 1915, when she was thirty-three. Few literary debuts have been more fraught with self-doubt, self-consciousness, ambition and dread. Louise DeSalvo identifies nine more or less distinct revisions of the text,[3] and a tenth was to follow for the American edition of 1920. (In 1929, for the Uniform Edition she and Leonard published at the Hogarth Press, she returned to the 1915 text.) Work on the novel was interrupted by her collapses into despair and delusions, and was also interwoven with them. Her reworkings, additions and suppressions reveal a colossal anxiety, and an equally obsessive determination to continue at all costs. Under this pressure *The Voyage Out* took on — and still retains — a special, subjective atmosphere. Its air is tense with things not said (Terence Hewet tells Rachel, when they are struggling to know each other inside out after their engagement, that he's planning to write a novel called 'Silence'); and at the same time it is packed with possibilities. For instance, Woolf excised or buried almost all reference to Rachel's dead mother, who figures large in early versions. But she also enhanced the allusions to larger patterns which link the dead with the living, and minor characters with major ones. Now, in the long second paragraph of Chapter 24, Rachel muses:

> Perhaps, then, everyone really knew as she knew now where they were going; and things formed themselves into a pattern not only for her, but for them, and in that pattern lay satisfaction and meaning. When she looked back she could see that a meaning of some kind was apparent in the lives of her aunts, and in the brief visit of the Dalloways whom she would never see again, and in the life of her father.

The invention of Clarissa Dalloway, round whom Woolf was to build the novel published in 1925, suggests how much of her distinctive fictional territory she was already laying claim to in *The Voyage Out*.

Since the publication in 1982 of the earlier draft called *Melymbrosia*, readers have been able to judge for themselves something of the scope of the transformations the book went through. The plot doesn't really change: in all versions Rachel goes to South America with her father and her uncle and aunt-by-marriage Ridley and Helen Ambrose. On the way, in Lisbon, they are joined for a brief but momentous stretch of the voyage (which includes one of the book's two storms) by the Dalloways, who debark on the coast of Africa. Once installed in the Ambroses' villa in the (imaginary) resort town of Santa Marina, Rachel meets the motley band of British tourists at the hotel, who include Terence Hewet and his Cambridge friend St John Hirst. Along with them, and her aunt, she accompanies an eccentric pair of primitive-art fanciers, the Flushings, on a trip up the river and into the jungle (the novel's second voyage). There, Rachel and Terence declare their love and become engaged. A couple of weeks later, after their return to Santa Marina, Rachel is stricken with 'fever' and dies, the second storm breaks and wears itself out, and we are left with the shocked but ultimately inattentive chorus of hotel guests shuffling off to bed, and (soon) back to England. Rachel has had her 'season', she has 'come out' like a dubious debutante, and died of it somehow. But though these events remain the same, the style and structure alter a great deal. In *Melymbrosia* Rachel is a more easily likeable and more conventional heroine than the one we encounter later. She talks more, and more to the point; her naïvety and her openness to impressions take the form of enthusiasm rather than bafflement; she has already had one proposal of marriage; her relationship with Helen Ambrose is much more frank and loving; and Terence sees her as a 'free soul . . . That's why our life together will be the most magnificent thing in the world!' As a result, her death, in this version, is very hard to make sense of, unless you assume that a 'free soul' must necessarily soar or sink out of the world.

The trouble is that this Rachel, though perfectly moving and interesting, is not heroic enough to justify such a hypothesis. True, there are hints of a metaphysical scheme at work. Rachel intuits 'the presence of the things that aren't there . . . Her quarrel with the living was that they did not realise the existence of drowned statues, undiscovered places, the birth of the world, the final darkness, and death.' She 'wanted her mother', and she loves 'the sea and music because they don't die'. In short, she questions the finality of the material world: '. . . does it never strike you . . . that the great procession, these people we see going about, scattered everywhere without any connection, and you and me – we are not real, we cannot touch each other. And the present is only an instant.' But when she herself joins the unrealities and becomes one of the things that aren't there, it feels like a failure of narrative grammar, as though she has been, very unfairly, *taken at her word* just as she was about to resolve her 'quarrel with the living'. If you read *Melymbrosia* in the context of Woolf's life, however, the picture looks different. Her mother's death and her father's ten years later had both precipitated breakdowns; in between her half-sister Stella Duckworth had died just three months after her marriage, in 1897; her brother Thoby had died of typhoid after their return from a holiday in Greece, in 1906; and in 1907 her sister Vanessa, to Virginia's initial dismay, married Clive Bell. In her own experience the conventional either/or (death or marriage) that constituted the choice of ending for so many novels looks heavily weighted towards death. And in any case, the two may not have struck her as so dissimilar: we now know that she had been sexually abused in childhood, and in adolescence, by her Duckworth half-brothers, so that physical intimacy seemed to her a contradiction in terms. Helen in *Melymbrosia* indeed thinks, on Rachel's engagement to Terence, 'of marriage . . . of the sordid side of intimacy, of the wrench and the nakedness'. From this angle, the happiness of Rachel's engagement leads logically to death rather than consummation (she has the intimacy, and is saved from 'the sordid side'). One can begin to see a little more clearly why the novel was rewritten so agonisedly and so often.

The form of *Melymbrosia* was too traditional to articulate such wholesale ambivalence about marriage, about people's relations to their bodies, and about the structure of a character or a self. Woolf seems to have known this at the time. There is a moment early in the draft when we're told that for the housekeeper Mrs Chailey 'the family was everything': 'if Rachel one day put her child in Mrs Chailey's arms, she would feel as the keen novel reader feels when the story reaches its gorgeous climax, and ends happily, and one drops off to sleep, content'. The sardonic tone ('gorgeous climax') is a sign of Woolf's contempt for happy endings. They send you to sleep. Jane Austen sends Mr Dalloway to sleep in Chapter 4, though that may be a judgement on him. Conventional novels promise continuity, they re-produce a world. By the time of the final revisions of *The Voyage Out* for the British edition, Virginia had married Leonard Woolf (1912), and they had come to a decision that, given her instability, she would make books, but not babies.[4]

Before turning to the present text, there is one more ingredient in its prehistory that should be mentioned. It is clear (and Woolf's letters in some cases say as much) that many of her characters were based on real people. Thus, Helen Ambrose resembles her much-mythologised mother Julia Stephen, and (more closely) her sister Vanessa ('At lunch I compared you with a South American forest, with panthers sleeping beneath the trees'[5]); Mrs Dalloway is based on Kitty Maxse ('almost Kitty verbatim; what would happen if she guessed?'[6]); scholarly, demanding and (in many ways) helpless Ridley Ambrose has shades of her father Sir Leslie Stephen; St John Hirst is based on Lytton Strachey; Mrs Flushing perhaps on Lady Ottoline Morrell, 'who has the head of a Medusa; but she is very simple and innocent in spite of it, and worships the arts';[7] and Terence Hewet on Clive Bell, though possibly latterly also on Leonard Woolf. Rachel herself we might expect to be a portrait of the artist. In *Melymbrosia* Richard Dalloway asks, 'Are you sure you haven't got a novel up your sleeve, Miss Vinrace?' But in fact, though Woolf may have started off using herself as a model, the distance between them grows into a gulf. A letter of 1901 sounds very like the beginnings of Rachel:

> The only thing in this world is music — music and books and one or two pictures. I am going to found a colony where there shall be no marrying — unless you happen to fall in love with a symphony of Beethoven ... This world of human beings grows too complicated, my only wonder is we don't fill more mad-houses: the insane view of life has much to be said for it — perhaps it's the sane one after all ...[8]

By 1913, however, Woolf was sharing out her subjectivity

among other characters (including, despite his masculine origins, Terence) and developing her distinctive sense of where the novel as a form should go. Rachel becomes inarticulate, and even more the musician.

There were in any case many literary antecedents for what Henry James called 'the conception of a young woman affronting her destiny'. In his Preface to *Portrait of a Lady* he asks himself ironically why such 'presumptuous girls' matter — 'what is it open to their destiny to *be* . . . that we should make an ado about it?' Their slightness as subjects, for him, is precisely the point. The 'mere young thing' challenges one's intelligence and vision. Seen rightly, she is a vehicle for civilised passion; she carries other people's meanings, and symbolises the affective life that underpins continuity:

> George Eliot has admirably noted it — 'In these frail vessels is borne onward through the ages the treasure of human affection.' In 'Romeo and Juliet' Juliet has to be important, just as in 'Adam Bede' and 'The Mill on the Floss' and 'Middlemarch' and 'Daniel Deronda', Hetty Sorel and Maggie Tulliver and Rosamund Vincy and Gwendolen Harleth have to be . . .

George Eliot's metaphor makes the young woman a treasure-ship. Woolf, turning the image round, makes the steamer on which Rachel sails 'a bride going forth to her husband, a virgin unknown of men'. She knows the symbolic shorthand very well, for *The Voyage Out* is the work of an addicted reader (she'd also, since 1904, been a reviewer). Terence Hewet, we're told in Chapter 22, 'read a novel which someone else had written, a process which he found essential to the composition of his own'. Woolf's subject has a family tree which includes

James and Eliot, and stretches back to the Brontës, Elizabeth Gaskell, Jane Austen, Fanny Burney and Samuel Richardson, and forward, in the generation before her own, to a whole gallery of problematic heroines like Hardy's *Tess of the D'Urbervilles* or Meredith's *Diana of the Crossways*. Some set-pieces in *The Voyage Out* – particularly the picnic excursion in Chapter 10 and the dance in Chapter 12 – beg to be compared to Austen's scenes from genteel life in *Emma*. And, of course, the book is full of references to books of all kinds, from Austen and the Brontës to Balzac and Ibsen to Gibbon and Burke to Milton and Shelley, and Sappho and Pindar. Ridley Ambrose is editing Pindar, and he is draped throughout in the mystique of Greek, which patently stands for the preserve of male learning, while his wife Helen is content to *look* Greek while she does her needlework (and manages Ridley's life for him), and his niece Rachel is absorbed in her music, and given reading lists by the young men. It's worth recalling in the context of this splendid stereotyping that culture in the Stephen family had never fitted the conventional pattern: 'I write in the mornings and read Pindar', Woolf wrote in 1907; '. . . Adrian . . . spells out Wagner on the piano.'[9] One of the novel's strategies is to make Rachel (as far as literature is concerned) a *tabula rasa* – a mental virgin on whom others are tempted to impress their tastes. Tory politician Richard Dalloway recommends anti-revolutionary Burke, St John Hirst lends her his hero Gibbon's *Decline and Fall*, and Terence is reading Milton's *Comus* to her when the first symptoms of her illness appear. Rachel is a 'vessel' in more senses than one. People want to form her and 'bring her out'. Woolf on the other hand is interested in trying to get at what is formless and undecided in Rachel. Which is perhaps another way of saying that Woolf is searching for her own style, trying to write her way past the accumulated meanings that literary tradition had loaded on to young women.

The Voyage Out is openly nostalgic for a past when the world looked new. The crossing to South America provides a pretext for imagining Elizabethan voyagers in the 'new world', back at the wide-eyed, heroic beginnings of colonial history: 'three hundred years ago five Elizabethan barques had anchored where the *Euphrosyne* now floated. Half-drawn up upon the beach lay an equal number of Spanish galleons, unmanned, for the country was still a virgin land behind a veil.' We're told that the appearance of the river is 'what it was to the eyes of Elizabethan voyagers'; and as they penetrate into the jungle, Hewet, 'staring into the profusion of leaves and blossoms and prodigious fruits', says, 'That's where the Elizabethans got their style.' 'Dashing' Evelyn Murgatroyd at the hotel, who is a kind of privateer of the emotions, always undecided between the various men at her feet, has several exasperated outbursts on this subject:

'Oh how I detest modern life,' she flung off. 'It must have been so much easier for the Elizabethans! I thought the other day on that mountain how I'd have liked to be one of those colonists, to cut down trees and make laws and all that, instead of fooling around with all these people who think one's just a pretty young lady. Though I'm not. I really might *do* something.'

Evelyn M. plans to go next to Moscow, where she's heard there's a revolution brewing. The interesting thing here is that 'modern life' means a life dense with inhibitions and traditional structures. Modern life is like Rachel's aunts' drawing-room, crammed with Victorian furniture, views of Venice, reproductions of Italian paintings, and family portraits: a world tamed and cluttered, in which you bump up against icons of 'taste' and respectability everywhere you turn. Modern life is indefinably old, it's hard to believe in the new. Mrs Flushing has a try, however, and absurd as she is, she voices something of the novel's frustration with its inheritance: 'Mouldy old pictures, dirty old books, they stick 'em in museums when they're only fit for burnin'.' Her enthusiasm for contemporary painting, combined with her husband's investment in primitive artefacts, represents one version of modern*ism* (set against modern life).

Woolf looks a lot further back than the Elizabethans in exploring what beginnings involve. For instance, when Rachel obediently reads Gibbon, what she sees to start with is not the Enlightenment irony or the neoclassical balance, but something quite else, magic words (Arabia Felix, Aethiopia, barbarians, forests, morasses) which 'seemed to drive roads back to the very beginning of the world . . . the book of the world turned back to the very first page'. Later Gibbon dies on her, but 'the infinite distances of South America' themselves are working on her imagination in the same way. This is a world where roads and maps and (European) narratives of progress and expansion have a very limited purchase; the earth is 'like the immense floor of the sea', it is partitioned into countries, and cities grow, but on the long view 'the races of men changed from dark savages to white civilised men, and back to dark savages again'. As the small party embark for the book's second voyage up the river they are travelling in time, into a primeval forest where they seem to be 'walking at the bottom of the sea'. Here Terence and Rachel declare themselves, against a background that cruelly emphasises their self-consciousness. In the native village that marks the end of their journey the whole party feel themselves 'treading cumbrously like tight-coated soldiers among these soft instinctive people'. The villagers first stare them out, then ignore them, and they feel chilled and somehow rebuffed. Helen Ambrose is troubled by vague premonitions of disaster when she sees how awkward and vulnerable the English look in this alien landscape.

Woolf here is registering the gradual change in ways of seeing brought about by Darwin. In supplying humans with a pre-human prehistory, he had opened out time and shrunk its recorded portion. Early on in the novel we find Rachel 'haunted by absurd jumbled ideas – how, if one went back far enough, everything was intelligible; everything was in common; for the mammoths who pastured in the fields of Richmond High Street had turned into paving stones and boxes full of ribbon and her aunts'. This vision is wonderfully comic and surreal: it reminds one that there were many different ways of taking Darwin, and that Woolf for her part saw evolutionary theory as putting the solid, 'real', modern world into a different focus. *The Voyage Out* has sometimes been compared with Conrad's *Heart of Darkness*, but they have in the end little in common, since for Woolf it's not the primitive that awakens horrors. The horror that lurks in Rachel's nightmares is at the heart of civilisation. The village in the jungle just *is*, it symbolises nothing, and that is its strangeness for characters whose lives are plagued by a plethora of signs and representations. Woolf seems to have thought of modern cultures as evolving by means of more and more elaborate codes of differentiation – race, gender, language, class, generation, and so on and on. Her own way of imagining a beginning, and making it new, involves super-imposing a lateral (synchronic) continuity on a linear (diachronic) model, mammoths in Richmond High Street. All the watery imagery signals her desire to imagine a common matrix, some element in which you can 'solve the limits of fields'. Life came out of the sea, after all.

So she ships the English to Santa Marina, and deprives them of 'the supporting background of organised English life', so that they are seen in high relief. The Dalloways *en route* provide a foretaste of the effect, though they are much more grand socially speaking than any of the other characters, and assume their right to speak for England, despite the humiliations of seasickness. The hotel guests are variously middle class, and they are indeed highly differentiated. St John Hirst (himself quintessential Cambridge) labels them 'all types . . . you could draw circles round the whole lot of them, and they'd never stray outside . . . Mr Hughling Elliot, Mrs Hughling Elliot, Miss Allan, Mr and Mrs Thornbury – one circle . . . Miss Warrington, Mr Arthur Venning, Mr Perrott, Evelyn M. another circle; then there are a whole lot of natives; finally ourselves.' ('Natives' here are Portuguese colonists.) Hirst's rudimentary social map is drawn on the basis of generation, of marital status, and of respectability, so that, for example, his first circle encloses the middle-aged and old, those whose sexual destiny is fixed (Miss Allan is a professional woman, a confirmed spinster). His second group encloses the unmarried, but also those who are in one way or another insecure: Susan Warrington fears she'll spend her life as a poor relation minding richer ones, for example, and Mr Perrott is so impeccably gentlemanly that people infer (correctly) that he is a self-made man, from humble origins. As if to emphasise the sense of their all being on a stage, stuck in their roles, we first encounter the hotel people when Helen Ambrose and Rachel eavesdrop on them, looking in from the dark garden – 'Each window revealed a different section of the life of the hotel.' And this scene is pointedly reversed later when Hewet walks up to their villa in the dark, and listens in on Helen and Rachel. This motif underlines the gaps between people, how far they're 'in the dark' about each other – particularly men and women, who seem sometimes almost like animals of different species.

Rachel at the villa (the division of space is always important in this novel) has been brought up by the Richmond aunts in near-total ignorance of sex, and is only gradually and painfully coming to terms with the 'facts' and – much more important – the psychological and cultural assumptions that are concealed in the conventional destiny of love-and-marriage. Hewet and Hirst talk between themselves in a blasé and sometimes brutal fashion, but it turns out that they too, Hirst especially, are peering nervously across a gulf. 'Cambridge', the misogynist, rebarbative, rationalist Cambridge ethos, is the shorthand for their condition. One example of the resulting tone will suffice: 'What I abhor most of all . . . is the female breast.' This is Hirst. Hewet didn't stay the course at Cambridge, and perhaps partly for that reason he is very much interested in other people. He becomes the novel's go-between, organising the picnic that first tempts people out of their grooves, and looking into their lives with curiosity and imagination. Hewet *empathises*. He develops a kind of androgynous insight into women's experience, and it's he who describes to Rachel how patriarchal attitudes work:

'The respect that women, even well-educated, very able women, have for men,' he went on. 'I believe we must have the sort of power over you that we're said to have over horses. They see us three times as big as we are or they'd never obey us . . . It'll take at least six generations before you're sufficiently thick-skinned to go into law courts and business offices. Consider what a bully the ordinary man is . . . the daughters have to give way to the sons; the sons have to be educated; they have to bully and shove for their wives and families, and so it all comes

45

over again. And meanwhile there are the women in the background . . .'

He points out to Rachel (surely there is irony here?) that women's experience is unrepresented, circumscribed and silenced. Their talk becomes intensely important to both of them: you could almost say that they get engaged in order to have an uninterrupted conversation. And yet there is a radical asymmetry in their relationship. In acquiring Rachel, Hewet is completed, he'll be a better novelist – 'the world was different, it had, perhaps, more solidity, more coherence, more importance, greater depth'. Whereas Rachel retains an impersonal, inchoate want that provokes him to say jealously, 'There's something I can't get hold of in you.' Her vague dissatisfaction, which she cannot really articulate ('she wanted many more things than one human being – the sea, the sky'), constitutes a passive protest against the life that awaits them back in England. England, in the novel's structure, represents the past *and* the future: marrying, they'll be going *back*. Evelyn M., contemplating them, thinks, 'Love was all very well, and those smug domestic houses, with the kitchen below and the nursery above, which were so secluded and self-contained, like little islands in the torrent of the world.' Hewet, addressing Rachel in imagination, says 'I'd keep you free', and again the ironies close in.

People like the Dalloways are the ones in charge of the England that awaits Hewet and Rachel. Richard Dalloway is a 'man of the world', energetic, opportunist, overbearing, very much the politician, hard-headed yet sentimental when it suits him. His wife Clarissa worships him (she imagines him, grotesquely, as a type of Christ), and supplements his 'mission' with charm, social grace, culture – though not too much – and snobbery. They are a perfect example of the assignment of separate spheres to men and women. Clarissa entrances inexperienced Rachel; Richard condescends to explain his programme, and – when the storm buffets them together into her room – kisses her passionately. The nightmare images of sexual revulsion he calls up (echoed later in her dying delirium) connect Dalloway with the theme of 'no return'. This finished version of *The Voyage Out* makes Rachel's death seem less romantic, more ironic and ambivalent – as though by dying she's passing judgement on the type-cast and compartmentalised life that's in store for her. She won't be a 'vessel' carrying the culture's codes, and reproducing its values. John Bayley has suggested that 'Rachel dies, in effect, so as not to become a "character"'.[10] It's a reading that makes a great deal of sense, though his further argument that Woolf, wishing 'to avoid having to take part in an art form shaped and dominated by the masculine principle', denied herself 'the free make-believe of the masculine world' is a lot more questionable. The traditional novel of character didn't strike Woolf as 'free make-believe'. It was for her, already, at her setting out, a travesty of freedom, a set of conventions that denied life its complexity and fluidity. What Bayley is really saying is that he sees the new novel Woolf was working towards as a kind of anti-novel.

In fact, she was renewing the forms of fiction, looking towards the future. For example: her dissolution of 'character' anticipates the experiments of French 'new novelists' thirty years later. Nathalie Sarraute in particular was to jettison '"types" of flesh and blood human beings' for 'carriers of . . . unexplored states of consciousness, which we discover within ourselves'.[11] Sarraute's first novel was not a 'portrait of the artist' but *Portrait of a Man Unknown* and there are interesting analogies here with *The Voyage Out*, in the impatience with the limits of the self, and with definition in general. A much later Sarraute novel, *Fools Say*, describes what she and Woolf both dreaded as artists:

> Everybody what they are. Clinging completely to themselves. Entirely justifying their designations and qualifications. Sweet little old women. Exquisite old men walking their dogs with the look of a dog. Lovers embracing on benches . . .

To such writers the traditional novel looks like a preserve of *unfreedom*. Woolf's refusal to make Rachel a 'vessel' for established meanings starts, paradoxically, to look like a sign of life – even though she dies. There are deaths and deaths. Roland Barthes in *Writing Degree Zero* in 1953 put it this way: 'The Novel is a Death; it transforms life into destiny, a memory into a useful act, duration into orientated and meaningful time . . . It is society which imposes the Novel . . .'[12] Woolf's own statements along these lines are well known. In her 1919 essay on 'Modern Fiction' she says that 'if a writer were a free man and not a slave . . . there would be no plot, no comedy, no tragedy, no love interest or catastrophe in the accepted style . . .' *The Voyage Out* is a voyage of exploration.

It contains all sorts of hints of what's to come. Terence and Rachel reappear (with a gender-change) as Clarissa Dalloway and Septimus Smith in *Mrs Dalloway*: the party-giver and the lost soul, aspects of a continuous consciousness. And the dissolution of the boundaries of individual selves in all the later fiction is anticipated here in the way in which the most unlikely characters, at certain moments, speak a language of unity. Even Richard Dalloway, all unawares, joins in when he advises Rachel to 'Consider the world as a whole'; hearty Arthur Venning is briefly transfigured ('I seemed to see everything . . . As if it had a kind of meaning'); Mr Bax, the commonplace clergyman, hits on the metaphor of 'the myriad drops that compose the great universe of waters'; and disaffected Hirst ends contemplating the hotel guests 'half-asleep, yet vividly conscious of everything around him', and forgets for a while his contempt. Because *The Voyage Out* was so long-gestated and had its origins in such personal materials, critics have often been tempted to treat it as symptomatic evidence of Woolf's life-crises. But Thomas Caramagno is more to the point when he sees the book as a 'translation' or 'transformation' of her experience.[13] In any case, manic-depressives, he argues, face mood-swings that seem to come from nowhere (probably hereditary neurohormonal imbalance), so we should not look back into personal history for causes. Whether he's exactly right or not about the nature of her illness, the emphasis he puts on *what she made of it* is crucial. In Woolf's first novel 'things formed themselves into a pattern' that was to change the map of fiction, and not only for her. One result of that change is that meanings become freer and more fugitive. And because she is bent on measuring her distance from the conventions, you get the sense that you can see her at work, making a place for herself.

Notes

1. *The Letters of Virginia Woolf*, ed. Nigel Nicolson and Joanne Trautmann, 6 vols. (London: Hogarth Press, 1975–84), I.223.
2. *Letters*, I.438.
3. Louise DeSalvo, *Virginia Woolf's First Voyage: A Novel in the Making* (London: Macmillan, 1980).
4. The ambivalence about her sexuality was not resolved by

her marriage: see Roger Poole, *The Unknown Virginia Woolf* (Cambridge: Cambridge University Press, 1978), still probably the best analysis of the interrelation of this aspect of the life and writing.

5. *Letters*, I.574.

6. Ibid., 342.

7. Ibid., 487.

8. Ibid., 35.

9. Ibid., 381.

10. John Bayley, 'Diminishment of Consciousness: A Paradox in the Art of Virginia Woolf', in Eric Warner (ed.), *Virginia Woolf: A Centenary Perspective* (London: Macmillan, 1984).

11. Nathalie Sarraute, 'From Dostoievski to Kafka' (1947), in *Tropisms and the Age of Suspicion*, trans. Maria Jolas (London: John Calder, 1963), pp. 75–6.

12. Roland Barthes, *Writing Degree Zero* (1953), trans. Annette Lavers and Colin Smith (New York: Hill & Wang, 1981), p. 39.

13. Thomas Caramagno, 'Manic-Depressive Psychosis and Critical Approaches to Virginia Woolf's Life and Work', *PMLA*, 103 (1988), 10–23.

III

KATHERINE MANSFIELD

The Garden Party

Fables and fairy tales are age-old and used to be passed around by word of mouth, but short stories are a modern invention and reflect something of the loneliness of the acts of writing and reading. With the modernist movement in the early years of the twentieth century, the form took on a particularly obsessive character, and writers like Katherine Mansfield (and James Joyce and D. H. Lawrence) made short stories into intensely crafted and evocative objects-on-the-page, sometimes with nearly no plot at all in the conventional sense. Katherine Mansfield put even more into the story form than her contemporaries, however, since it was really her *only* form. She sometimes regretted this – she joked that Jane Austen's novels made 'modern episodic people like me ... look very incompetent ninnies', and said to an old friend, sadly, at the end of her life, that all she'd produced were 'little stories like birds bred in cages'. But her very dissatisfaction feeds into her stories, and gives them a special edge. And in any case, her pleasure in the form is clear. She felt at home in it, being so little at home anywhere else.

She left well-to-do New Zealand society behind in 1908 at the age of nineteen, but she remained something of an outsider in English literary circles. Her contacts with the people she met were eager, tense, competitive and mutually mistrustful. Most women in this world were helpmeets or patrons or

53

muses or mistresses, not artists in their own right, as she wanted to be. And even in literary Bohemia the old social distinctions died hard. She was a colonial and her banker father was a self-made man, so that she fitted all too well into a certain ready-made snobbish stereotype: 'provincial', 'trade'. It's possible to recapture something of the impact she made on English sensibilities by looking at her relations with the one major woman writer she knew well, Virginia Woolf. Their on-off friendship was marked by conflicting feelings of alienation and intimacy. A diary entry by Woolf for 1917, after she and Leonard had had Mansfield to dinner, reads:

> We could both wish that ones first impression of K.M. was not that she stinks like a — well civet cat that had taken to street walking. In truth I'm a little shocked by her commonness at first sight; lines so hard & cheap. However when this diminishes, she is so intelligent & inscrutable that she repays friendship.

Even if you make allowance for Woolf's habitual private savagery, this passage shows what a powerful physical presence Mansfield had. Pioneering Mansfield scholar and biographer Antony Alpers was puzzled by Woolf's overreaction. Katherine, he said in his 1980 *Life*, liked expensive French perfume (and dressed very well, for that matter). Perhaps the Woolfs thought it vulgar to wear scent at all? Alpers concluded that it must have been Mansfield's passion for 'the life of the senses' that offended Woolf's sensitive nose.

He was putting it too mildly. That 'civet' reference is to the secretions of the musk glands of a cat, once upon a time an ingredient for making scent. Woolf was probably thinking of Shakespeare's *As You Like It*, where bawdy Touchstone explains

(Act III, scene 2) that sweet-smelling courtiers who use civet aren't as clean as they seem, because 'civet is of a baser birth than tar, the very uncleanly flux of a cat'. Put the implications together and Woolf is saying – with a sort of fascinated disgust – that Mansfield is like a tom-cat marking out its territory and (at the same time) a she-cat on heat. And, of course, the social and sexual messages are mixed up, too, so that the 'lines' of her personality seem 'hard & cheap'. Yet in the next sentence she's transformed into someone 'intelligent and inscrutable', a new kind of aloof and attractive cat who has an inner life. This was a sentiment Woolf repeated in a diary entry of 1920: 'she is of the cat kind, alien, composed, always solitary & observant'. When she thought of Mansfield in this way Woolf felt very close to her: '. . . we talked about solitude, & I found her expressing my feelings as I never heard them expressed'. She felt, she said, 'a queer sense of being "like" – not only about literature'; 'to no-one else can I talk in the same disembodied way about writing'. And Mansfield wrote to her in a letter of that same year: 'You are the only woman with whom I long to talk work.'

Looking back in 1931, some years after Katherine's death, Virginia wrote to Vita Sackville-West:

I thought her cheap, and she thought me priggish, and yet we were both compelled to meet simply in order to talk about writing . . . she had, as you say, the zest and the resonance – I mean she could permeate one with her quality; and if one felt this cheap scent in it, it reeked in ones nostrils . . .

It's as though, as soon as she thinks about Mansfield, even eight years dead, she catches that shocking feral smell on the air: of the sexual adventuress, the stray cat, so disturbing because they

55

shared the same dedication to writing. Katherine was a rival writer, not someone's girlfriend. Woolf liked, as she said, to talk about work in a 'disembodied' way, but Mansfield's body wasn't so easily dismissed.

We know how she struck another rival writer and sometime friend, too, for D. H. Lawrence based the character of Gudrun in *Women in Love* at least in part on Mansfield. In the spring of 1916 Lawrence, Frieda, Katherine and her lover (later husband) John Middleton Murry had rented next-door cottages in Cornwall. They lived in great emotional closeness too. Katherine, in a letter to a mutual friend, Koteliansky, famously provided an eye-witness account of one of Lawrence's murderous rows with Frieda ('Suddenly Lawrence . . . made a kind of horrible blind rush at her . . . he beat her to death . . . her head and face and breast and pulled out her hair') and the even more horrid spectacle – she implies – of their reconciliation afterwards: '. . . next day, whipped himself, and far more thoroughly than he had ever beaten Frieda, he was running about taking her up her breakfast in bed and trimming her a hat'. Lawrence, Claire Tomalin argues in her biography of Mansfield, *A Secret Life*, made Gudrun very like Katherine in general – 'gifted artistically, charming, spirited, a good talker, a bit of a feminist, a bit of a cynic . . .' – as well as putting actual incidents from the period of their friendship into the novel. By the time *Women in Love* was finished, she and Murry had disappointed Lawrence, by refusing to fit into his plans, particularly Murry, with whom he imagined making a male bond of brotherhood. Claire Tomalin suggests, though – gruesomely but plausibly – that the real blood-bond (*Blutbrüderschaft*) was the one Lawrence formed unknowingly with Katherine: he may have infected her with the tuberculosis that killed her, since he was already suffering from the disease, though he died later than she did.

Woolf and Lawrence in their very different ways reflect the force of Katherine Mansfield's personality, her gift for closeness and her sly separateness, too. She was an object of speculation and gossip and jealousy, and she often gave as good as she got. The philosopher Bertrand Russell, with whom she flirted in 1916, wrote that 'her talk was marvellous . . . especially when she was telling of things she was going to write, but when she spoke about people she was envious, dark and full of alarming penetration' (*The Autobiography of Bertrand Russell*, Vol. II, London, 1963). The hostility to her, as a species of adventuress, was very real. You can, though, catch more inward and tender glimpses of her in the work of her contemporaries. Tomalin points out that Lawrence's portrait of Gudrun includes passages which peer inside her head when she lies sleepless in the night as Katherine often did, 'conscious of everything, her childhood, her girlhood, all the forgotten incidents, all the unrealised influences, and all the happenings she had not understood, pertaining to herself, to her family, to her friends, to her lovers, her acquaintances, everybody. It was as if she drew a glittering rope of knowledge out of the sea of darkness . . .' (*Women in Love*, Ch. 24). If this is Katherine, she must have talked eloquently to Lawrence about her past, 'telling of things she was going to write . . .' For as time went by she did indeed turn for inspiration more and more to the world she had left behind, across a 'sea of darkness', the New Zealand of her childhood and adolescence. In this collection, in fact, nearly half of the stories have a New Zealand setting, including 'The Garden Party' itself and 'At the Bay', which has pride of place as the opening story.

It is appropriate that 'At the Bay' comes first. Along with 'Prelude' (1917, collected in her earlier book, *Bliss and Other Stories*) and 'The Aloe', a longer, messier, early version of 'Prelude', it represents Katherine Mansfield's fragmentary and extraordinarily vivid account of her origins and of her family, the Beauchamps – renamed Burnell in the stories. 'At the Bay' is set in Karori, four miles outside Wellington; the Beauchamps moved there when Kathleen Mansfield Beauchamp, as she was christened (Mansfield was her maternal grandmother's maiden name), was four and a half years old. The move was a sign of her father's success and growing prosperity – Harry Beauchamp was already well begun on the brilliant business career that would make him a prominent figure in the colony's commercial life, leading to directorships of many companies, and (eventually) the Chairmanship of the Bank of New Zealand and a knighthood. Kathleen was the third child. The fourth, Gwen, died as a baby, and after the sixth, Leslie, the only son, there would be no more, probably because Annie Beauchamp (like Linda Burnell in the story) had a 'dread of having children', and so stopped after producing the necessary boy. Certainly she didn't dote on her offspring any more than her fictional counterpart. She went with her husband on a long trip to Europe when Kathleen was one, and in general the mothering was left to *her* mother, Granny Dyer.

Kathleen, the middle child, was plump, intense and bespectacled, and maybe more trouble than the rest – though the evidence for that may have been informed by hindsight, when she became the family's black sheep. The first innocent step in that direction was in 1903 when, along with her two older sisters, she was taken to England for the first time, and enrolled in Queen's College, Harley Street. It was an expensive school that offered a very good education, one of the best available for girls then, and there she became absorbed in music, literature, fashionably 'decadent' taste (Wilde in particular) and passionate friendships. She wrote for and later edited the college magazine, learned the cello, and fell in love with London – or at least

London as reflected in the paintings of Whistler. She began to see herself as an artist, though it wasn't clear at all which art she meant. And (perhaps most important) she formed a connection that would be life-long with Ida Baker, who'd also had a colonial background, being born in Burma. This wasn't a lesbian relationship – though people sometimes thought so – but a kind of surrogate sisterhood, or even marriage (Mansfield actually referred to Ida as a 'wife', not exactly a term of affection for her). Ida would over the years become companion, nurse or servant when required, and would retreat into the background whenever Mansfield didn't need her. She was needed a lot, and much resented for it. Nonetheless, it may be said that if Kathleen/Katherine discovered the beginnings of her vocation at Queen's College, she also discovered, in Ida – whom she later renamed Lesley Moore, 'L.M.' for short, a pseudonym to complement her own disguise – the person who would supply the support that made it possible for her to produce her best work.

From her family's point of view, however, her superior London education was not at all meant to lead to a career; it was designed to fit her for a superior style of domestic and social life, and in December 1906, at eighteen, she returned according to plan to New Zealand. As it turned out, it was too late: she had become a native of elsewhere. In the words of biographer Claire Tomalin, 'something more than the sense of being at home in Europe was stamped on her ... this was the habit of impermanence. The hotel room, the temporary lodging, the sense of being about to move on, of living where you do not quite belong, observing with a stranger's eye – all these became second nature to her between 1903 and 1906.' Certainly, once home in Wellington, she became outrageously and unmanageably discontented. And now there were lesbian affairs – or at least one: she re-met and flirted with glamorous Maata, a Maori 'Princess' she'd first known as a girl; and was passionately, physically in love with Edith Bendall, an artist and illustrator in her twenties.

She was full of loathing for the Beauchamp world – 'Damn my family . . . I detest them all heartily' – and she began to stand back from it, and see it with vengeful coldness, as a confidence trick on women:

> Here then is a little summary of what I need – power, wealth and freedom. It is the hopelessly insipid doctrine that love is the only thing in the world, taught, hammered into women, from generation to generation, which hampers us so cruelly. We must get rid of that bogey . . .

By 'love' she meant love-and-marriage, of course. Simone de Beauvoir in *The Second Sex* (1949) would quote Mansfield's autobiographical Beauchamp stories with special approval, for the clarity with which they identified the mystificatory processes that entrap women. She picks out a passage from 'Prelude', where the unmarried sister Beryl (based on Mansfield's young aunt Belle) admires her own guitar-playing, as a splendid example of the way 'the romantic desire for a woman's destiny' is fuelled by narcissism and the cult of self. And from 'At the Bay' Beauvoir quotes at length the passage where Linda Burnell thinks about her husband and the doubtful meanings of 'love' – including her dread of having children – and concludes that Mansfield as good as demonstrates 'that no maternal "instinct" exists'. The stories refuse to honour conventional sentiments – that is part of their modernity, and their courage and distinctiveness. Beauvoir said rather solemnly that this was because Mansfield looked at her characters in the light of their 'total situation'. Another writer, Willa Cather, had put it more expressively: 'I doubt whether any contemporary writer has made one feel more keenly the many kinds of personal relations which exist in an everyday "happy family" who are merely going on living their daily lives . . . every individual in that household (even the children) is clinging passionately to his individual soul, is in terror of losing it in the general family flavour' (*Not Under Forty*, 1936). With the young Kathleen/Katherine, this 'terror' became so acute, and so uncomfortable to everyone else, that in 1908 she was allowed to do as she wished, and leave once more for London, after eighteen months of 'home'.

She would never return, except in imagination. But before she became the woman who could write up the Beauchamps in this fashion, and turn them into the luminous characters of her fiction, she would have many adventures. Before she really became a professional writer at all, indeed, she herself lived rather like a character in a book – though in her case, it was as the heroine of a picaresque novel, 'modern' and 'episodic' to excess. An account of her first year and a bit will set the tone of her new life. On arrival she more or less adopted the musical Trowell family, known from New Zealand, but her affair with the son, Garnet, foundered on his parents' disapproval. In a bizarre gesture of defiance, in March 1909, she married a mild-mannered English admirer with artistic hobbies, a man she hardly knew called George Bowden, and left him on their wedding day to join Garnet, who was in the orchestra of an opera company touring the provinces. In May (by now she was pregnant) her mother arrived in London, carried her off to a Bavarian spa town, left her there to have the baby, returned to New Zealand, and briskly cut her disgraceful daughter out of her will (her father, however, would continue to send her an allowance during her life). Meanwhile Katherine had a miscarriage, collected material for stories by observing her fellow guests, and wrote to Ida Baker asking her to send her a child to look after, which Ida duly did (an eight-year-old boy called Charlie Walter, who was recovering from pleurisy, and who was sent back at the end of the summer, having served his purpose). She now met Floryan Sobieniowski, a Polish writer and translator who introduced her to Chekhov's stories; they had an affair, and she contracted the gonorrhoea which – unrecognised and untreated – would give her agonising rheumatic pains for years, and probably made her infertile. By the beginning of 1910 she was back in London (with the help of a 'loan' from Ida) and had produced a story freely adapted (some would say plagiarised) from Chekhov, 'The-Child-Who-Was-Tired', which was published in the magazine *The New Age* edited by A. R. Orag, who also printed a story called 'Germans at Meat'. She settled on the name Katherine Mansfield, in life as well as on the page. Her writing career had begun.

It was small wonder that Woolf scented an adventuress. For Mansfield the years between 1908 and 1918 were hectic, crowded with people and restless with movement. By 1918 she had become seriously and unmistakably ill with TB, and had just begun to produce her best work – '*grown up* as a writer', as she put it. She'd lived like someone on the run, an escapee from the prisons of respectability, making up her life as she went along, often disastrously, but at least the mistakes were *hers*. There is no room here for a blow-by-blow account, but two people in her history must be singled out, since they represent (apart from Ida) the nearest thing to continuity she could bear to claim: her second husband John Middleton Murry, and her brother Leslie Beauchamp.

Mansfield met Murry in December 1911, in March the following year he became a lodger in her flat, and shortly afterwards her lover. He was a year younger than she in literal fact, but a lot younger in other ways: a clever, charming, ambitious young man, making his own way in the world from humble origins, via Oxford, where he founded a short-lived little magazine called *Rhythm*, on which she joined him as a co-editor. They seem to have been surrogate siblings to each other: playfellows, chums and allies. Though he was a would-be novelist at the beginning, his was a critical sensibility, and it was as an editor, reviewer and critic that he would make his name, for the most part after her death. Their eventual marriage, after her divorce from Bowden in the spring of 1918, makes them sound a more settled couple than they were. Many commentators, looking back on Mansfield's life-story, have found Murry wanting. He was slippery, restless, indecisive, unreliable and seldom at her side when she needed him. On the other hand, it's hard not to feel that – having made the running from the beginning – she continued the relationship less out of passion for him than out of a failure of energy and nerve. She was too ill and time was too short to go on the prowl any more.

Her brother, Leslie 'Chummie' Beauchamp, was twenty-one when he arrived in England in February 1915 to join up. After a spring and summer in officer training-school, he left for the Front in France in October, and a few days later he was killed in a grenade accident, 'blown to bits' in Katherine's words. During their reacquaintance she had lied to him merrily about her relationship with Murry: 'more than ever in love', Leslie wrote to their parents. In fact, they were on the verge of parting company, and to prove the point and assert her independence, Katherine made her own excursion to the Front, unknown to Leslie. She went to join a lover, Francis Carco, a novelist of the Parisian underworld, and a friend of another writer–adventuress, Colette, and she succeeded in outwitting the military to join him for a brief idyll, which she described in her journal.

In a sense, this has little to do with her relations with her brother, except that, with both Leslie and Carco, what is striking is her sense of the man as a double, a kind of lover/brother, an other self. Describing going to bed with Carco, she focuses on his prettiness ('one hand with a bangle over the sheets, he looked like a girl'), and their talking and laughing together under the bedclothes: 'lying curled in one another's arms . . . A whole life passed in thought. Other people, other things.' Their resemblance was perhaps increased by the fact that she seems to have chopped off her hair on the way as a vague 'disguise'. As for her real brother, again they were said to look very alike, and according to her biographer Alpers, Leslie was known to contemporaries as rather a 'pansy'. After his death, she wrote to him in her journal: 'You know I can never be Jack's lover again. You have me. You're in my flesh as well as in my soul.' Though she and Jack were reconciled once more, she did make dead Chummie into a kind of Muse: 'The next book will be yours and mine. It is the idea that I do not write alone. That in every word I write and every place I visit I carry you with me.' He was one of the reasons why she turned more and more to New Zealand memories, and he is also a character in some of those same stories: a new-born baby – but already a charmer – in 'At the Bay'; the real-life original of the ideal brother whose very name mirrors the heroine (Laura/Laurie) in 'The Garden Party':

'. . . But Laurie –' She stopped, she looked at her brother. 'Isn't life,' she stammered, 'isn't life –' But what life was she couldn't explain. No matter. He quite understood.

'*Isn't* it, darling?' said Laurie.

These famous last words of one of her best-known stories are, of course, thoroughly ambiguous, and include an element of mockery. But that only means that – characteristically – Mansfield was critical of her own longing for closeness, someone 'in my flesh . . . in my soul'. Any Muse of hers could not be all sweetness and light. Indeed Alpers thinks that Leslie also lurks behind spoiled Harold in 'An Ideal Family', the despair of his father: 'too handsome by far; that had been the trouble all along. No man had a right to such eyes, to such lashes and such lips; it was uncanny.'

Mansfield seems to have felt that her own vocation as a writer was vindicated in Leslie's death: she could immortalise their shared childhood world somehow, carry on the family 'line' in the way only an artist can. That he was not aggressively masculine, may have been bisexual or gay, underlines their closeness. He was on her 'side' somehow, also an outsider. Carco too lived on in her fiction, in no very flattering fashion. Mansfield scholars generally agree that she borrowed his voice, and something of his feline knowingness, in creating Raoul Duquette in her 1918 story '*Je ne parle pas français*', one of the first in which she found her own distinctive voice. Maybe in the end Katherine Mansfield's bisexuality was not so much a matter of sexual practices (there's no evidence of sexual relationships with women after her teens), but of what went on inside her head, the character of her creative self.

Like almost all her important work, '*Je ne parle pas français*' was written outside England, at the various resorts and refuges she visited in search of kinder weather and better health. She was increasingly driven by her illness, and subject to despair and rage. She wrote to Murry from the South of France, in November 1920, in this vein, scorning his long-distance praises and desperate for his real attention:

I don't want dismissing as a masterpiece ... I haven't anything like as long to live as you have. *I've scarcely any time, I feel* ... Talk to me. I'm lonely. I haven't ONE single soul.

D. H. Lawrence, himself very ill but refusing to know it, raging on his own account, sent her a horrible letter – 'He spat in my face and threw filth at me, and said: "I loathe you. You revolt me stewing in your consumption."' Curiously, perhaps because of her own volatile and terrible temper, she doesn't seem to have found this as devastating as one might expect. And in any case, she was *not* alone, for she had L.M. (Ida Baker), though all too often L.M. didn't quite count except as an object of disgust and resentment. The very physical resilience and stolid *presence* on which Mansfield relied also drove her to ecstasies of hate: 'Her great fat arms, her blind breasts, her baby mouth, the underlip always *wet*, and a crumb or two or a chocolate stain at the corners – her eyes fixed on me – fixed – waiting for what I shall do so that [she] may copy it ...' Nevertheless it worked, and she worked. By the time her first major collection, *Bliss and Other Stories*, was published in 1920 she had already begun on the next, *Garden Party* stories, at the Villa Isola Bella in Menton.

In fact two of these stories, 'The Young Girl' and 'Miss Brill', are actually set on the French Riviera, and feature characters from the endlessly shifting, motley, rootless population of towns like Menton. Mansfield's immediate surroundings weren't a major stimulus, though: she was working largely with themes and materials she had squirrelled away in her memory. However, it is rash to generalise about her processes of composition, as one particular example, 'The Daughters of the Late Colonel', will demonstrate. One of the germs of this story, Antony Alpers was able to show, is found in a scribbled note interpolated in the manuscript of 'The Young Girl', a monologue from L.M. which Mansfield seemingly took down verbatim, as it was uttered: '"It's queer how differently people are made," observed L.M. "I don't believe you could understand even if I told you . . . And it isn't as if there were anything to explain – if there was I'd understand – anything tangible, I mean. But there it is, I've always been the same from a child . . . out of my depth in the big waves – or when I'm walking along a dark road late at night . . ."' This she made over into Constantia's closing meditation in the story, with its marvellous evocation of misgivings, signs misread, a life let slip. She began 'The Daughters of the Late Colonel' in late November 1920, and finished it in a marathon session on 13 December: '. . . at the end', she wrote in her journal, 'I was so terribly unhappy that I wrote as fast as possible for fear of dying before the story was sent'. When she finished it, late at night, L.M. provided egg sandwiches and tea. Like the other stories, it was published first in a magazine, in this case the *London Mercury*: Mansfield had no difficulties now in placing her work, and did not rely only on the *Athenaeum*, which Murry edited, though she was as always short of money. One group of the *Garden Party* stories was written for the *Sphere* magazine, at ten guineas each – 'Mr and Mrs Dove', 'An Ideal Family', 'Her First Ball', 'Marriage à la Mode' and 'The Voyage'. She worked on these with great speed, and in some cases it shows, in the rather pat shapes, and stagy effects. But again, it's wrong to generalise, since 'The Voyage' is as fine-tuned and suggestive as the best of her late writing.

She was writing against her body's clock in any case, and this pressing sense of urgency is always felt in the work. Her very experimentalism – the way, for example, her narrative voice speaks through one character after another, her refusal to take a secure, generalising overview – is itself informed by her impatience. There's no *leisure* to generalise, and no place to stand to take the broad, panoramic view. Claire Tomalin describes the effect very well: 'The particular stamp of her fiction is the isolation in which each character dwells . . . there is no history in these stories, and no exploration of motive. The most brilliant of them are post-impressionist . . . grotesquely peopled and alight with colour and movement.' The tone is not sad or depressed, often the reverse. She wrote in a letter to Murry from this period from Menton, that 'suffering, bodily suffering such as I've known . . . has changed for ever everything – even the appearance of the world is not the same – there is something added. *Everything has its shadow*.' This shadow serves to heighten the colours, and sharpen one's awareness of the present moment. Her very lightness of touch, in fact, and her economy with description and analysis can themselves be read as signs of her changed sense of her bodily self.

The craft of writing is what's left to her, and the pleasure of the text becomes a kind of secular salvation. What's not said is frequently as vital as what *is* said – if she assumes the voices of different characters, she also takes possession of their silences, when they catch their breath and run out of words. Critics have registered this curious cross-infection of her illness and her style, sometimes in slightly macabre ways. So, for example, Claire Tomalin calls the work 'short-winded'; and even someone who starts from the texts rather than from the life, like feminist critic Kate Fullbrook, will write, 'her characters' identities are riddled with gender codes as if with an unshakeable disease . . .' (*Katherine Mansfield*). And, of course, death is more or less openly a theme in the *Garden Party* stories, a terrible and tasteless event that can't be allowed to intrude on the land of the living, but does all the time and everywhere. 'The Stranger', a story which pays a kind of homage to James Joyce's 'The Dead' from *Dubliners* – a salute from one modernist to another – marvellously casts death as a most accidental acquaintance. Mr Hammond (based on Harry Beachamp, and so boyishly energetic, possessive, hopeful) chafes at the delay on the quay as he waits for his wife's boat to dock, bringing her back from a trip to Europe. When she does arrive, he is ardent, proprietorial and – such is their relationship – aware as always that she holds something of herself back. This time, though, the 'something' takes on more definition than usual, for she tells him that the cause of the delay was that a passenger died, and he died in her arms. It's as though she'd confessed to a ship-board romance, but much worse. She has embraced the enemy that keeps people separate for ever, the fact of their deaths. This is why he can't own her, and why for all his striving he can't, in the end, compete. It's a frightening and blackly funny story – and it may in part have been inspired by a hidden set of family facts. Mansfield's parents had had a similarly shadowed meeting in 1909 in Hobart, Tasmania, though the 'stranger' had been buried at sea; perhaps even more to the point were her mother's death in 1918 and her father's marriage eighteen months later to his dead wife's closest friend, Laura Bright, one day after disembarking from the boat at Auckland – for all the world as if, faced with death, he did everything he could to deny it.

The resulting story stands on its own, of course – and it also interacts in the reader's imagination with the others in the collection. Mansfield may have been too breathless – or simply too 'episodic' and 'modern' in her whole view of narrative – to settle to writing a novel, but she did create a different kind of continuity made up of allusions, cross-references and affiliations among the separate stories in the book. They were, in other words, open-ended not only in the sense that they frequently tail off on her characteristic note of questioning, evasion and bad faith (see the ending to 'The Garden Party' quoted on page 64), but also in the sense that they suggest each other. One example is the very theme of death, which itself develops a weird continuous life from one story to another: in 'The Daughters of the Late Colonel' the death of Con's and Jug's mother is associated in their minds with the black feather boa round her neck in her fading photograph; the boa links across to Miss Brill's pathetic fur-piece, which 'dies' when she is mocked by a couple of young lovers in the public gardens. When she puts it back into its box, she links with another image, the little girl and her Grandma in their tiny cabin on the boat in 'The Voyage' – a cabin a bit like a coffin, though the child's mother's death, the reason for the trip, is never directly mentioned. And this 'box' takes one back to the blackly comic sense the daughters of the late Colonel have that he is somehow still living in the chest of drawers, or the wardrobe.

Associations of this kind are evanescent, unreal, created in the process of reading and re-reading. Now you see them, now you don't. But that temptation to read between the lines is again a modern and modernist effect. It is a way, perhaps, of implying a shared world of meanings without exactly mapping it out, or giving it solidity. Mansfield's stories come together rather as people come together in some public place – the park, the square, the theatre, or indeed at a party, which is why she chose the right title for the book. Leonard Woolf, sounding less dismayed than Virginia, said, 'By nature, I think, she was gay, cynical, amoral, ribald, witty . . .' (*The Autobiography of Leonard Woolf*). By which he implied that the tragic accident of her illness and early death, at thirty-four in 1923, had turned her against her real grain. It's impossible, of course, to tell whether this was so. However, it is striking that some of the best brief critical notes on her, by other women writers, have refused to see her as a figure of pathos, but emphasised instead her bloody-mindedness. Thus Brigid Brophy in a piece for the *London Magazine* in 1962 contrived to imply that her death from consumption was somehow self-created, a kind of turning inwards of her *consuming* passion: 'Katherine Mansfield had indeed a cannibal imagination . . . When Katherine Mansfield refused to undertake a proper cure for her illness, she was acting out what she had written years before as a healthy but wrought-up adolescent: "I shall end – of course – by killing myself." The disease through which she did kill herself was consumption . . . the cannibal disease which consumes its victim . . .' This seems far too late-Romantic a view. Mansfield was not a prototype for Sylvia Plath, she absolutely didn't want to die young. However, one can appreciate Brophy's motive, which is, somehow, to make sense of Mansfield's suffering, make it an active act, not a passive thing. Another writer who praised Mansfield along similar lines, for her aggressiveness, was Angela Carter: 'one of the great traps for the woman writer is the desire to be loved for oneself as well as admired for one's work, to be a Beautiful Person as well as a Great Artist, and Katherine Mansfield was only saved from a narcissistic self-regard by the tough bitchery under her parade of sensitive vulnerability' *(Nothing Sacred)*.

This tone brings one back to Woolf's response to the rival writer – and yet the intimately recognisable writer – marking out her distinctive territory. *The Garden Party and Other Stories* was Mansfield's last book. She was too ill even to complete many individual stories after it was finished: the rest of the short time she had left was spent in an increasingly desperate search for cures and miracles. At the very end she joined a bizarre, visionary commune in Fontainebleau, run by the Russian guru Gurdjieff, a kind of eccentric circus which gave her some peace at last. It was an improbable version of belonging, but it served. In her work she was and remains one of the great modernist writers of displacement, restlessness, mobility, impermanence. The very vividness of her New Zealand writing bears this out. She wanted, she said, 'to make our undiscovered country leap into the eyes of the Old World . . . It must be mysterious. It must take the breath.' Her own words are in the end the best introduction – she wrote so well about writing, since she invested the life she wouldn't see again in it: 'All that I write – all that I am – is on the borders of the sea. It is a kind of playing.'

The Notebooks: Vols I–II

These handsome volumes contain the last remains of Katherine Mansfield: a full and final transcription of the amorphous mass of hopeful notes, dissatisfied jottings, bad poems, sick scribbles, lists, sums and drafts, some dating back to her youth, which she left behind when she died in January 1923. All her bits and pieces are here, chronologically arranged and beautifully bound, with a picture of the cheap exercise books she used on the cover, their faded marbled fronts transformed into a bookish reliquary.

This was the material John Middleton Murry mined for the selections he called the *Journal* and the *Scrapbook*, though it's long been known that there was no such distinction. Margaret Scott, who is also co-editor of the five-volume Mansfield *Collected Letters*, has worked for years on these Mansfield papers at the Turnbull Library in Wellington, New Zealand, where most of them are kept (the rest are in Chicago), and where she was a librarian. The long toil involved in deciphering their unreliable handwriting and arcane order must suggest a labour of love. Is Ms Scott perhaps the archival equivalent of Mansfield's much abused lady minder 'L.M.' (Ida Baker)? Not in the least. Some of Mansfield's own witty and acerbic tone seems to have rubbed off on her. She takes a cool pleasure in pointing out, for instance, that one of the *mots* Murry salvaged – 'Spring comes with exquisite effort in England' – actually reads 'Spring comes with exquisite effect . . .', which is much less original. And her line on punctuation is distinctly interventionist. Instead of preserving Mansfield's careless, impatient dashes, she has changed them in the interests of readability:

> In the early notebooks she was scribbling so fast that the only form of punctuation she used was a dash. A dash was quicker and easier to make than a backward-turning comma or a stationary full stop. As she wrote, at top speed, and 'heard' the need for a pause she employed a dash. Since many of these dashes function as commas or full stops I have rendered them so.

Where Murry supplied exclamation marks and question-marks to dramatise Mansfield's fervour, Scott renders her merely clear, wherever possible. This makes sense: these notebooks were not used to articulate an 'inner' rhythm, they were not another kind of writing – writing about writing – but a means to the end of work in the world.

More than anything Mansfield wanted to be an artist in the public sense. If the notebooks have an inward and reflexive dimension it's because for most of Volume I, which takes us up to 1914, she was an adolescent and an apprentice – 'I have a perfectly frantic desire to write something really fine, and an inability to do so which is infinitely distressing' (1908) – and for much of Volume II, which covers the years until her death, she was ill with TB, and often artificially and unwillingly isolated. In fact, one of the most interesting aspects of her jottings is that they question the assumptions we make about the nature of people's interiority, and particularly about writers' inner lives. Mansfield notes jokily on some loose leaves dating from around 1920 that nowadays selves are two a penny, we seem to have hundreds of selves: 'what with complexes and suppressions, and reactions

74

and vibrations and reflections – there are moments when I feel I am nothing but the small clerk of some hotel without a proprietor who has all his work cut out to enter the names and hand the keys to the wilful guests'.

What this means, however, is that the quest for the elusive one true self is becoming more urgent than ever before: 'Is it not possible that the rage for confession, autobiography, especially for memories of early childhood is explained by our persistent yet mysterious belief in a self which is continuous and permanent.' Her tone is ambivalent, for she too found herself going back, in her New Zealand stories. And yet she's agnostic about the continuous self. It's typical of her to see the act of writing in the foreground, forming the one identity or the many. Reviewing novels for the *Athenaeum* she complained, in a letter to Murry: 'I am amazed at the "mushroom growth" of cheap psychoanalysis everywhere. Five novels one after the other are based on it; it's in everything . . . these people who are nuts on analysis seem to me to have no subconscious at all. They write to *prove* – not to tell the truth.' Instead she trusts to her own 'queer hallucinations', the stories she writes 'straight off'. The notebooks do contain drafts, but they are mostly false starts or failed ideas. For her best and best-known stories there are hardly any studies, sketches, early versions. To write well, it seems, she needed to cheat her own self-consciousness and abolish introspection.

She is just the opposite, in other words, of the other great woman modernist she knew, Virginia Woolf, for whom diary-writing, notes and letters – all the words that form the hinterland of the books themselves – were an intimate part of the creative process. Living and writing merge for Woolf, she lives literature, and over the years the books become more and more shapelessly like the letters and diaries. But for Mansfield, who found her voice on the page at almost the same moment that she became seriously ill, living doesn't bear thinking about too closely, she wills to work. In one of the most revealing and memorable passages here, from late on, in 1921, she ponders the function of solitary scribbling:

> Queer this habit of mine of being garrulous. And I don't mean that any eye but mine should read this. This is – *really private*. But I must say nothing affords me the same relief. What happens as a rule is, if I go on long enough *I break through*.

Another habit is Dickens. She is always asking Murry to send a saving Boz novel she hasn't yet read to her sickbed in the South of France, and among her complaints about the contemporary fiction she reviews is that 'the writers (practically all of them) seem to have no idea of what one means by continuity . . . they introduce their cooks, aunts, strange gentlemen and so on, and once the pen is off them they are gone – dropped down a hole.' Continuity for her is invested in illusion. In one letter to Murry she says she 'dare not keep a journal': 'As a matter of fact I dare not tell the truth . . . The only way to exist is to go on and try and lose oneself – to get as far as possible away from this moment. Once I can do that all will be well. So it's stories or nothing.'

We're probably programmed now to read these remarks as though she could have afforded to be a better person, more confiding and open with herself and other people, if it hadn't been for her terminal illness. But it's imaginatively more plausible to see her as forced into even this degree of self-commentary by cultural quarantine. She was trapped into immanence, privacy, stewing in her own juice: by temperament and choice she was interested in doing, not being, a self-made woman with (as Woolf noticed sniffily) 'hard' outlines, smart scent and a squared-off Louise Brooks fringe. There was no fun in writing about writing. Perhaps the most famous entry of all in these papers is the one where she records her first haemorrhage – and also her dread of not having enough time to assemble an oeuvre:

February 19th 1918
I woke up early this morning and when I opened the shutters the full round sun was just risen. I began to repeat that verse of Shakespeare's: 'Lo here the gentle lark weary of rest' and bounded back into bed. The bound made me cough. I spat – it tasted strange – it was bright red blood. Since then Ive gone on spitting each time I cough a little more. Oh, yes, of course I am frightened. But for two reasons only. I dont want to be ill, I mean 'seriously' away from Jack. Jack is the 1st thought. 2nd I don't want to find this is real consumption, perhaps its going to gallop – who knows – and I shan't have my work written. *Thats what matters*. How unbearable it would be to die, leave 'scraps', 'bits', nothing real finished.

It's no insult to the authenticity of her terror to see that this is a set-piece. Her impulse is to write it up – a 'scrap' more eloquent than most, but still in her terms 'nothing real', since for her 'real' means crafted, delivered, structured, new.

Driving herself on to write her 'real' work, she populated her solitude with spooks, surrogates and scapegoats. Her brother Leslie (Chummy), blown to bits in an accident with a grenade in France in 1915, had become a Muse and mentor: 'Dear brother as I jot these notes I am speaking to you . . . I see you opposite me.' His presence ('when I leaned out of the window I seemed to see my brother dotted all over the field – now on his back, now on his face, now huddled up, now half pressed into the earth') is already a reminder of how short the time really is: 'This year' – 1916 – 'I must make money and get known.' She is born again out of Chummy's death, she is the 'new man'; 'I do not write alone . . . I carry you with me.' Or again, out of her disappointment and resentment against Murry for not being with her, not playing Muse, writing complaining letters about money, she produces a phantom brain-child: 'If one wasn't so afraid – why should I be – these aren't going to be read by Bloomsbury et Cie – I'd say we had a child – a love-child & its dead . . . J. says forget that letter. How can I? It killed the child – *killed* it really & truly.' And Ida Baker, L.M., who does look after her, she makes into a nanny and a 'ghoul': 'the smallest cough and her soft voice asks did you speak. Can I do anything.' Thinking of the visceral hatred she could find in herself for L.M. – large, hungry, strong, slow – she sometimes cast her in the role of fat Frieda, and herself in the role of skinny D. H. Lawrence, whose rages she now recognised all too well. This comes out more, though, in the letters to Murry, where he is meant to feel at once flattered by her violent revulsion against L.M., and accused (since he should be the one living in dangerous, devoted intimacy with her and her eminently infectious disease). In the notebooks she is often relatively restrained, for want of an audience. Margaret Scott comments that Murry must nonetheless have had a bad time transcribing some of this stuff: 'Are you really, only happy when I am not there? . . . Now, I feel in your letters . . . you are breathing again . . . yes, Ive a *shrewd* suspicion.' (He's callous enough to breathe freely when she's exiled, when they're together he's in an anguish of anxiety, perhaps even selfish anxiety, not wanting to breathe the same air.)

However, she didn't dissipate too much precious energy on anger. She was always trying to work, scribbling until something 'real' started to materialise. In the feverish, fertile years 1917 and 1918 it's as though she's trying out other people's voices – ones that didn't exist in literature yet, but turned out to belong to other adventurers and colonials, to Christina Stead, or Jean Rhys. This passage, for instance, is surely a first draft for *Good Morning, Midnight*:

> Thank God! the steps have gone past my door. In the mirror she saw again that strange watchful creature who had been her companion on the journey, that woman with pale cheeks and dark eyes & lips whose secret she shared, but whose air of steady desperation baffled and frightened her and seemed somehow quite out of her control.

And Christina Stead's man who loved children is a close relative of the father in a fragment titled 'Love – Lies – Bleeding':

> The children loved their father when he began to talk like that. He would walk up and down the room, holding his coat-tails out for a skirt, laughing and jeering at women and at their imbecile unbelievable vanity. The children used to sit at the table and bang with their fists and clap their hands and jump up and down.

The echoes from the future suggest the many-sided writer she might have been as a novelist – though her penchant for one-off 'hallucinations' might anyway have kept her faithful to the short story as a form.

In her stories she could (and regularly did, between 1917 and 1921) pull off the illusionist feat of storing infinite riches in a little room, creating a sense of physical and moral space – relations of class and sex writ large, but with endless subtlety. She got her wish: she became part of the canon, a set book. And yet she is not these days our favourite kind of modernist, and the notebooks – because of what's not in them, because of what they don't reveal – suggest why. She doesn't write enough about her inner life, and when she does she often seems theatrical or ironic, or grotesquely sentimental (there are days during her enforced holidays on the Riviera when she lavishes significance on every baby bird, stray kitten, snail and lizard rash enough to wander into her garden). In any case she doesn't have the style of inner life that flatters our sense that all writers are striving towards the formless, the evasion of ends and the deconstruction of finalities. Her impending death, as with so many artists in those long centuries before life expectancy took off, made her in love with literature's promise of immortality, its returns on itself, its representations of wholeness and its freakshow of Life. This isn't a matter merely of wanting to belong to the great traditions of high culture, either. A 1915 diary entry reads: 'Went to Pantomime. Very interesting. Began to think of Panto tradition. Would like to write in it.'

In the event, she was trapped on her sofa like the lady of sensibility she wasn't. On Easter Monday in 1919, when she and Murry were living briefly in Hampstead, Virginia and Leonard Woolf visited, and they all went to the fair on the Heath. She wrote to Virginia: 'Never again . . . I felt there was nothing to do but sit on the stairs & lift up ones voice and – weep for Babylon. Were human beings in the mass always so shocking . . . ?' Virginia wrote: 'We thought she would have enjoyed herself from the likeness of her prose to the scene; on the contrary she was disgusted.' In fact the story 'Bank Holiday' in the *Garden Party* collection went on to do exactly what the

Woolfs imagined, so either Mansfield was putting on a voice for Virginia or, as often happened, her physical frailty made her resent and fear other people's jostling and noise. At all events she went back for more at Whitsun, and wrote (this time to Ottoline Morrell): 'On Bank Holiday, mingling with the crowd I saw a magnificent sailor outside a public house. He was a cripple; his legs were crushed . . . On his bare chest two seagulls fighting were tattooed in red and blue.' The 'Bank Holiday' story takes the same kind of pleasure in the spectacle of other people's performances, and her own. In another letter to Ottoline she describes a dinner party at around the same time, with Roger Fry as their guest: Roger 'thinks that Virginia is going to reap the world. That, I don't doubt, put on my impatience. After a very long time I nearly pinned a paper on my chest. "*I, too, write a little*."' Virginia has fulfilled Fry's prophecy. Her writing – and especially her endless self-commentary, her writing about writing – gratifies alike the present's love of biography and gossip, and its most radical cultural-historical theories. Her nostalgia for formlessness makes writing a story of potential, of the always unacted. Whereas Mansfield's work speaks about what's irretrievably lost, material, mortal, unless it is turned to artifice – and nowhere more than in these notebooks, where she is so reluctantly introspective.

IV

JEAN RHYS

After Leaving Mr Mackenzie

People are beasts when you're down, thinks good sister Norah in a rare moment of despair and rebellious hatred, but her bad sister Julia, the heroine of *After Leaving Mr Mackenzie*, just wishes that human beings *were* a fraction as direct and decent as the wild animals caged in the zoo. She wishes too that she hadn't had to sell her own fur coat: 'She began bitterly to remember the coat she had once possessed. The sort that lasts for ever, astrakhan, with a huge skunk collar . . . People thought twice before they were rude to anybody wearing a good fur coat, it was protective colouring, as it were . . .' In her fur she'd smell of money and have the power of seeming self-possession. But she has lost caste, slipped down the food chain until she resembles a meek herbivore.

When a hotel pageboy tells her Uncle Griffiths there's a lady to see him, he does so with the telling hint of a grin – '"A lady?" said Uncle Griffiths, in a voice which sounded alarmed or annoyed, as he might have said "A zebra? A giraffe?"' And when her uncle dismisses her with a pound, Julia finds herself out on a bleak London street where there's a drunk or a busker singing in the distance, in a voice that 'dragged and broke – failed. Then suddenly there would be a startlingly powerful bellow, like an animal in pain . . . not fierce or threatening, as it might have been; it was complaining and mindless, like an animal in pain.' Julia, who's in her thirties and has a 'past', now looks not so much old as fatally, shamefully vulnerable and worse for wear. Her face is 'round and pale with deep, bluish circles under the eyes', and her 'very thick dark hair was lit by too red lights and stood out rather wildly round her head'. Not only does she henna her hair, she makes up defiantly with powder, rouge and kohl on her eyelids, to disguise her growing panic. Painting her face to meet her sister over their mother's deathbed, she tells herself, 'Hurry, monkey, hurry.'

Jean Rhys has given to her creature Julia, who's reluctantly back 'home' from Paris and suffering from culture-shock, some of her own horrors when she first arrived in cold, dark England from the Caribbean. In *Smile, Please* (1979), her fragmentary and posthumously-published autobiography, she recalled how her aunt showed her the London sights in 1907:

> Westminster Abbey, Saint Paul's, the zoo ... We saw
> the lions first and I thought the majestic lion looked at
> me with such sad eyes, pacing, pacing up and down ...
> Finally we went to see the humming birds. The humming
> birds finished me ... Thick slices of bread smeared with
> marmalade or jam of some sort were suspended on wires.
> The birds were flying around in a bewildered way. Trying
> desperately to get out, it seemed to me. Even their colours
> were dim. I got such an impression of hopeless misery that
> I couldn't bear to look.

By the end of her long life Rhys had reduced her first impressions of England to these bare essentials – cathedrals and zoos, the guardian institutions of imperial civilisation. Though she did most of her writing in England, the places that made her *want* to write, the imaginary homelands that roused her imagination, were Paris, and her native Dominica. *Mackenzie* (1930) is a

Paris book, as were the two before it, *Quartet* (1928) and the 1927 collection of stories, *The Left Bank and Good Morning, Midnight* (1939). *Voyage in the Dark* (1934) and *Wide Sargasso Sea* (1966) were her West Indies books.

Julia in this novel is groping for a revelation which the cathedrals are not going to give her – a modern epiphany – and that's what Paris seemed to offer in the 1920s. There are traces of Dominica, though, on the text's horizon: in Julia's sense of being an exotic animal pacing baffled up and down her cage; and in odd, semi-private allusions, as when in a 'confusion of memory and imagination' she recalls 'a dark purple sea, the sea . . . of some tropical country she had never seen'. The plot makes a kind of realistic sense of this, when we learn that Julia's and Norah's mother had spent her childhood in Brazil, and though she's now near-speechless, and was always inarticulate about that past of hers, it's there in her blood and theirs. When Norah says vaguely, '. . . there's something wrong with our family. We're soft or lazy or something', she's evoking a colonial heritage (sensuous, careless, cut off, living above your means) that for a moment makes her and Julia seem truly sisters – until she remembers that she has done the proper thing and stayed home to nurse their mother, while Julia ran away.

Mother seems to Julia now to be about to utter some magic word or clue to their real lineage on her deathbed: she glares at her with what looks like recognition, mutters something – 'orange trees'? was she always sickening for that alien sun? – but she can't be sure. Most of the time mother is a whimpering lump on the bed, 'dark-skinned, with high cheek-bones and an aquiline nose'. Yet the strange thing, Julia thinks, is that she is still beautiful, 'as an animal would be in old age'. Her death has no power to unite her faded daughters, they quarrel savagely and childishly and nearly come to blows. All they're left with is their separate lives, and the uncertain future. Norah will now reap her reward and inherit what money there is, while Julia has only a cheap ring as a keepsake. Though perhaps there's something more – for as she leaves the flat she hears this time not an animal howling, but a barrel organ in the street –

To its jerky tune she tried to set words:

> Go rolling down to Rio
> (*Roll down – roll down to Rio!*)
> *And I'd like to roll to Rio*
> *Some day before I'm old!*

Later, when she's alone in her hotel room, the rackety tune still runs through her head, 'old' rhymes with 'gold', 'Great steamers, white and gold . . .' But she can't get it quite right, somehow.

It's a moment reminiscent, in its sentiment, its absurdity and its irony, of the kind of epiphany Katherine Mansfield had so exactly settled on in her last short stories, published in the early 1920s. In fact, her story 'The Daughters of the Late Colonel' was clearly an ingredient in Rhys's portrayal here of two sisters orphaned when it's nearly too late to grow up. A barrel organ in the street, to set nonsense-rhymes going in her characters' heads, is one of Mansfield's favourite devices too; and so is the dizzying, slightly nauseous feeling that you're teetering on the edge of a revelation that's just beyond your grasp. But strong though Mansfield's influence is, for a moment, Rhys escapes it and goes beyond it. Indeed, it almost seems as if, in *After Leaving Mr Mackenzie*, she is writing the sort of book Mansfield, with death around the corner, had no time for. In her *Journals*, which Rhys couldn't have seen, Mansfield jotted down ideas and scraps of narrative that sound eerily like Rhys. This passage, for instance:

Thank God! the steps have gone past my door. In the mirror she saw again that strange watchful creature who had been her companion on the journey, that woman with pale cheeks and dark eyes & lips whose secret she shared, but whose air of steady desperation baffled and frightened her and seemed somehow quite out of her control.

But whereas Mansfield, in her published stories, didn't explore further the panic of the woman alone, hunter and hunted – as she so often had been herself in Paris, as Rhys had been – Rhys has room in the novel to describe her character Julia's life in all its frightening and brutalising isolation, before and after this shared scene.

This is what makes *Mackenzie* a breakthrough book, as Carole Angier pointed out in her pioneering brief life, *Jean Rhys*, in 1985 – a 'turning point in [Rhys's] understanding of her fate'. She was plugging into her private experience, as she'd done in *Quartet*, but she was doing it with the lucid, 'uncompromising gaze' (Angier's phrase) of the deliberate artist. The book's title starts off as a lie – Mr Mackenzie left Julia, quite a while ago, and sends her a humiliating little remittance every week via his lawyer. But when the lawyer proposes to buy her off with one final payment, the pattern is broken, she is roused to rebellion, stalks Mr Mackenzie himself and confronts him in his local restaurant to tell him that she doesn't want his cheque. He's shocked and apprehensive – she must be even more crazy than he fears if she doesn't respect money – but instead of flying at him, she simply *shames* him with an absurd gesture out of romance:

A cunning expression came into Julia's face. She picked up her glove and hit his cheek with it, but so lightly that he did not even blink.

'I despise you,' she said.

'Quite,' said Mr Mackenzie. He sat very straight, staring at her . . .

And so she leaves him, and sets the plot in motion. Her quixotic gesture pays off almost immediately, for a stranger at another table, Mr Horsfield, is so struck by it that he follows Julia, and lends her the money that will enable her to go back to London and confront her disinheritance.

The restaurant scene in which Julia turns the tables on her ex-lover will bear further scruntiny, for it is full of surprising resonances. Mr Mackenzie seems comically paralysed by his own conventionality and lack of imagination. But in fact he is revealed as a cruel and calculating hypocrite:

He looked at Julia and a helpless, imploring expression came into his eyes. His hand was lying on the table. She put her hand on his, and said, in a low voice, 'You know, I've been pretty unhappy.'

At this change of attitude, Mr Mackenzie felt both relieved and annoyed. 'She's trying to get hold of me again,' he thought . . .

He drew his hand away slowly, ostentatiously. Keeping his eyes fixed on hers, he deliberately assumed an expression of disgust. Then he cleared his throat and asked, 'Well, what exactly did you want when you came in here?'

The word hypocrite (which we're told Mr Mackenzie always avoided 'as if it had been an indecency') derives from the Greek word for 'actor'. What's most interesting here, though, is that Mr Mackenzie is being shown behaving in exactly the way women are supposed to – teasing, leading her on, retreating into prudish distaste when she responds.

Had anyone written this scene this way before Rhys? Perhaps not. Certainly it went on being written the other way around, most famously by Simone de Beauvoir and Sartre, who honed their early existentialist analysis by watching people at restaurant tables, looking out for prize examples of what Rhys calls hypocrisy, and what they labelled 'bad faith'. A great deal can hang on how you read small bits of body language. This is a woman described in Sartre's *Being and Nothingness*:

> The young woman leaves her hand there, but *she does not notice* that she is leaving it. She does not notice because it so happens that she is at that moment all intellect . . . she shows herself in her essential aspect – a personality, a consciousness. And during this time the divorce of body from soul is accomplished, the hand rests inert between the warm hands of her companion – neither consenting nor resisting – a thing.

Beauvoir uses the same woman in her novel *L'Invitée*, published the same year as Sartre's book, 1943. Obviously they worked up the scene together. But what neither of them notices is that the man too is acting in bad faith, hinting at intimacy, but ambiguously, so that he can retreat into the role of friend if she doesn't respond. Though they cultivated an admirably unillusioned joint point of view, on the matter of whether men and women were equally guilty of *mauvaise foi* Sartre and Beauvoir were disappointingly traditional. Rhys by contrast is cruelly evenhanded.

Our point of view shifts continuously throughout the novel. We enter into the minds of many different characters as well as

Julia's, and can see how she too, from the outside, often seems insensitive: dishonest, fuddled with drink, callous, role-playing. Nonetheless, the new start she makes when shocked into taking stock does bring the world back to life – 'People were laughing, talking, pushing. Crowds of people were elbowing each other along a street, going to a fair . . .' The world takes on for a moment a carnival aspect, though it seems to be largely in her imagination, perhaps another of those phantom memories that belonged really to her mother and to another world: 'fair-music, vulgar, and yet lovely and strange'. And through her Mr Horsfield too starts to hope that he may live to see a little time in the sun before it's too late. One of the book's most intimate and moving moments – picking up the animal imagery and turning it to tenderness – is when he strokes her hair. He expects it to be hard and brittle, because he knows it's dyed, 'But in pushing it upwards it felt soft and warm, like the feathers of a very small bird.'

Rhys's people's thoughts are often given in quotation marks, a convention that stresses just how much they *don't* say, and how separate and out of step with each other they almost always are. Julia suffers time and again from a fear that she is unreal, that people can't hear her or see her properly. But although she thinks about her dead baby son and the break-up of her marriage when she goes to ask her wealthy first lover, Neil James, for money, she doesn't tell him about it. Only the reader gets to know. She tells Mr Horsfield how she once told the story of her life to a woman sculptor she used to sit for, pouring out her dreams, adventures and disppointments, looking all the while, as if in a mirror, at the woman in a reproduction of a Modigliani painting on the wall – and that when she came to the end the sculptor said, 'You seem to have had a hectic time', not having believed a word. She felt then as though her whole history had been stolen from her, that she was less alive than the painted woman, 'And it was a beastly feeling, a foul feeling, like looking over the edge of the world.' Julia, in short, is not the artist, but the model, she's not the soulful kind of woman who's supposed to make art, but the bodily kind who poses for it. And Rhys's originality is to make her real to us, particularly in moments like this when she doubts her own meaning. But although she is saved from insignificance, she is not saved from suffering or causing pain. Her fear of misunderstanding often becomes self-fulfilling, since she loses heart and feels too weary to explain herself. Brooding on the coldness she's felt and her loneliness, she ignores other people and tramples on their feelings. For example, Mr Horsfield's, whom she makes use of unmercifully, taking his sympathy for granted.

He – sounding in fact like a precursor of Sartre and existentialism – tells Julia, 'I think there's a good deal of tosh talked about free will myself.' She carries on with her monologue regardless, telling him how she told the unbelieving sculptor her history because 'I felt it was awfully important that some human being should know what I had done and why I had done it . . .' The layers of meaning here are dizzying indeed, like coming to the edge of the prospect of human communication. Rhys, like Mr Horsfield, thinks free will is probably tosh, but writing gives you a brilliant illusion of it. No wonder she was always such a reluctant writer – she seems to have feared you could never articulate 'the other side', the other point of view, because wherever you got to there was always another side.

After Leaving Mr Mackenzie doesn't even leave Mr Mackenzie behind, he's still there with his point of view, still managing to think well of himself, to the end. It's a novel poised between hope and despair. Later in the 1930s Jean Rhys enjoyed a song Jean Harlow sang, called 'Everything's been done before'.

'I like it very much', she told Francis Wyndham in a letter in 1964, 'and I sing it a lot – to my words – as the only other line of the original that's stuck is "But it's new to me – it's new to me."' In fact much of what she did as a writer hadn't been done before. The 1930s were a fertile time for her – not least because, despite her self-doubt and ingratitude, Mr Horsfield's original, Leslie Tilden-Smith (who became her second husband in 1934, and spent a small inheritance on taking her back to Dominica for a holiday), was acting as her typist, reader and literary agent. In her years with him she transformed her past into fiction, and turned the chorus-girl, the *demi-mondaine*, the something out of a zoo ('Norah kept looking at her as if she were something out of the zoo') into a real character to be reckoned with. Not that she merely added another specimen to the fictional repertoire: she changed something about characterisation itself, and the way she saw men like Mr Mackenzie, too, was new and strange. He joined the likes of Julia on the stage, in the cage. Perhaps the best way to start is to imagine Julia's 1920s Paris hotel room as a stage-set, a set on which respectable, solid assumptions were about to be taken apart. On the mantelpiece a picture, a still life left by the artist in lieu of payment. Along one wall, a red plush sofa – 'The picture stood for the idea, the spirit, and the sofa stood for the act', and the idea and the act themselves were as much a movable feast as the props.

V

CHRISTINA STEAD

The Salzburg Tales

The Salzburg Tales (1934) was Christina Stead's first published book, written, she said, with euphoric speed – written *out*, it almost seems, unpacked from the extraordinary imaginative baggage she'd brought to Europe from Australia. She was thirty-two. She'd first known she was a 'word-stringer' (her word) when she produced 'an essay, at the age of ten, on the life-cycle of the frog ... I remember the feeling of certainty' and the writing of the *Tales* struck her the same way:

> I wrote a story every first day of a pair, finishing it and putting in the connective tissue the second day; the third day starting another story ... I wrote *The Salzburg Tales* very fast and it gave me the same satisfaction I had with the History of the Frog; simple, complete, no questions asked. It doesn't often happen.

The result, though, is anything but simple. It's a kind of 'treasury' in the sense of the old anthologies, like *The Casket of Literature* ('twelve volumes with excerpts') she'd read as a child – a heady concoction of every style of story-telling she knew or could invent, rich and strange and overflowing with energy. Strange, above all. Her childhood and young womanhood had bred a mythomane. First, there were the stories she was told as a small, motherless girl by her father; then the stories she told her tribe of half-brothers and sisters – 'I used to rock them to sleep and talk them to sleep and tell them all the tales of Brothers Grimm and Hans Andersen. And towards the end, I made up stories for them.' In her brilliant autobiographical novel *The Man Who Loved Children* (1940) the adolescent heroine Louie relives some of this. She too 'towards the end' makes up stories – in particular one called 'Hawkins, the North Wind', a grotesque tale designed to distract everyone's attention from the obscene, terminal rows between her father and her stepmother:

> . . . the children lay loosely in the warm night; while things just as queer as *Hawkins* went on downstairs: Henny, of course, it was, not Hawkins shrieking, and Daddy was trying to give away Charles-Franklin . . .
> 'He is not mine!'
> 'He is yours, I've told you a thousand times.'
> 'How long was it going on?'
> 'Don't be a fool! I can't stand any more of it; I'll kill myself . . .'

The point here is that stories are at once a refuge and a kind of reflection of the fantastic, imprisoning reality of family life – all those disparate identities and desires jostling for space.

In Stead's accounts of herself, the creative impulse is always bound up with love and its opposite (she is a good hater), and with the mysteries of personality, and the difference of destinies. Louie at school is surprised into feats of fervid 'word-stringing' by unrequited love for her teacher, Miss Aiden –

> . . . and this was what came out:
> 'There was a wedding at the circus! The hermaphrodite

married the bearded, the giant the dwarf, the fat lady the hungry wonder, the clown in bags the lady in tights, the flea the elephant, the tiger a lily, the tent a Pole, the wind a Russian . . .'

The words cross-fertilise, cavort, contradict and reproduce themselves, in a labour of love. Many years later, in a 1982 interview with Giulia Giuffré, Stead, when asked 'What compelled you to write?' replied, 'I was born that way. I had no ambition. My ambition was to love . . . It's the same. Writing is creative, loving is creative. It's exactly the same.' One can begin to see how the elaborate format of *The Salzburg Tales* – the interwoven stories all told by different narrators sparking off ideas and images in each other – seemed 'natural' to her. A nearly contemporary interview reported in the *Australian Women's Weekly* spelled out her position rather more patiently:

> My purpose, in making characters somewhat eloquent, is the expression of two psychological truths: first, that everyone has a wit superior to his everyday wit, when discussing his personal problems, and the most depressed housewife, for example, can talk like Medea about her troubles; second, that everyone, to a greater or lesser extent, is a fountain of passion, which is turned by circumstances of birth or upbringing into conventional channels – as, ambition, love, money-grubbing, politics, but which could be as well applied to other objects and with less waste of energy.
>
> There are some whom this personal sentiment makes wanderers and some who stew all their lives in their own juice and ferment. I confess that the study of personality is a private passion, with me.

She had become one of the wanderers, and a writer, but she thought of her work as a shared enterprise. Hence her lifelong contempt for the merely literary, and the 'professional' – 'I don't associate with writers . . . I learn from human beings. Or even a cat, a hedgehog.'

Certainly, she hadn't exactly rushed into print. She had put together some stories in Sydney in the 1920s, but they hadn't found a publisher. The manuscript came along with her on her long-planned journey to Europe in 1928. When she arrived in London she wrote her first novel, *Seven Poor Men of Sydney*, which she showed to Marxist economist (and, as it happened, writer) William J. Blake, initially her employer, very soon her lover, mentor, husband. It was Blake who showed *Seven Poor Men* to Sylvia Beach in Paris (they were quickly on the move, as they were to be all their lives together); Sylvia Beach in turn suggested London publisher Peter Davies, and he agreed to take it, on condition Stead produced another book first. This was *The Salzburg Tales*: she remembered three stories ('On the Road', 'Morpeth Tower' and 'The Triskelion') from the earlier short story manuscript, which had by now been lost in her various moves, and wrote the rest at the bank in the Rue de la Paix where she was working. (The bank was remarkably tolerant: indeed bankers and businessmen, she claimed, were part of her inspiration, being compulsive *raconteurs*.) The 'frame' for the book – a motley group of tourists and music-lovers gathered in Salzburg for the festival, whiling away the intervals of Mozart by tale-telling – was modelled on Boccaccio's *Decameron* and Chaucer's *Canterbury Tales*; though her people are more whimsi-cally assorted and self-consciously diverse. 'What a company we are!' exclaims the swaggering lawyer from Budapest. 'We come from every corner of the earth: we have seen the world; we know Life. Let us amuse each other.' They are all 'somewhat eloquent' (as Stead wryly put it), all raised above 'everyday wit' by the occasion and the opportunity for revelation and speculation it provides. At the same time they share a curious equality, which provides a link between the *Tales* and the novel *Seven Poor Men of Sydney*: they act out Stead's conviction 'that everyone . . . is a fountain of passion'. They belong for the moment to a kind of magic democracy, where there's difference without hierarchy.

This effect is established at the very beginning, with the richly textured 'Prologue', and the intimate, malicious, fascinated descriptions of 'The Personages' which level everyone and everything *up*. For example, here is the Frenchwoman (compare Chaucer's Prioress):

> She was dressed in a costume of black and white silk in small stripes like hairs laid close together, with a belt of red leather and silver . . . when she took off her gloves, which were always clean, she had on a silver chased ring for a wedding ring and a platinum ring with a diamond as large as a shoe-button, for she thought she might one day have to fly in some sudden uprising of the farmers, or some political disorder in the south, or in war, or pestilence . . . She had been to Lourdes, to Lisieux and Rome and to all the famous places of pilgrimage . . . Yet she always had a tolerant smile for unbelievers and jested smartly with those who laughed at her piety . . . When she sat mistress at a table the wines were numerous, course followed course with succulent fleshes, subtle sauces and new garnishings, and compliment followed compliment with fresh blandishments . . .

The colours and textures, the animal, vegetable and mineral of the lady, are set out as if in a rich embroidery on the page;

the epicurean passage about food echoes Chaucer, and is also a humorous acknowledgement of the greedy sensuousness of the whole *ensemble*, words to be rolled on the tongue ('succulent', 'subtle', 'garnishings', 'blandishments') and caressed with eyes (or fingers?) – 'small stripes like hairs laid close together'. It's a description veined with irony, but devoid of judgement. Like the other 'Personages' the Frenchwoman has her nature, and that's that. The way this is done is, perhaps, evidence of another aspect of Stead's imaginative inheritance. The story-telling father was a naturalist (an expert on fish and fisheries) and she often later claimed to have been cured of any moralising urge by learning early to see the human world with a naturalist's eye (a trick that came in useful for standing up to father too): 'You don't say, "You bad sea-anemone, you shouldn't eat live things" . . . They *do* eat them and otherwise they wouldn't be alive and be like a lovely little flower.' All 'The Personages' are, as it were, sea-anemones, described with minute attention to their habits, distinctive markings and coloration, deceptive or otherwise. Stead's similes again and again link them with the natural world – a beautiful schoolgirl's ill-fitting skirt is wrapped round her 'like a chrysalis skin'; the Mathematician has deep blue eyes 'under brows like dried peony follicles'; a Berlin businessman has a 'bald cranium shaped like a sea-elephant's'; the Old Man's 'thin, bent head nodded every few minutes like a tremulous head of oats'; the Stenographer's arms are 'rough skinned as a shark's fin'. Also distinctive (and disconcerting, even occasionally surreal) is Stead's habit of writing about people's skin and hair and clothes and jewels as if they're *all* plumage, or scales: this Irishwoman, for instance – 'on her bare wind-blown neck, pitted with a web of goose-flesh, like shagreen, hung a plain gold cross . . .'

The stories they proceed to tell one might think of, carrying on the analogy, as curious secretions – snail-trails (say), or snail-shells, or spiders' webs; or birds' nests, or bee-dances. The comparison does help, up to a point, to suggest something of their idiosyncrasy, complexity and compulsiveness. They're of every known kind *except* the conventional realist sort Stead would have called 'professional' with its consciously modern greyness, its carefully managed, graded disclosures, its rationed ambiguity and sense of an ending. Nothing is rationed here. Only uniformity is in short supply, so that there is no story that can 'represent' the others. An inventory would list Gothic, romance, folk-tale, legend, fairy-tale, ghost-story, fable, anecdote, satire, joke, parody, and so on, and on. All 'The Personages', however reluctant, have a tale of sorts to tell. With some of them it's an addiction, second nature. For example, the Music Critic (not at all a nice piece of work) boasts of his powers of extracting meaning from the smallest signs:

If you have five minutes to observe a man, from a secret cranny, you will find out a great deal about him. Does he shake his head, loosen his collar, noiselessly gargle his throat . . . ? What are his half-dozen tics? . . . There are a thousand things to observe which will give away the party he votes for and the amount of his bank-balance. And for this reason, I am an inveterate and shameless eavesdropper, I listen at the doors of rooms, I pussyfoot along the corridors . . .

The most incorrigible, restless and inventive of them all, though, is the Centenarist ('a publicist . . . specialising in the centenaries of famous men') who acts as the author's *alter ego* – 'full of tales as the poets of Persia: he unwound endlessly his fabrics, as from a spool the silks of Arabia'. He is a cosmopolitan Jew, sceptical, sad, mischievous – a type Stead was to use again in her second novel, *The Beauties and Furies*, in the character of Marpurgo ('I'm a sort of fabulist, the Arabian Nights is my natural background'). Here, the Centenarist takes it upon himself to round off each day's story-telling with his own brand of tall tale concerning great rabbis, shamans, gurus and saints of all denominations. His tongue seems lodged firmly in his cheek, and his insidious, sometimes ribald suggestions about things holy and absolute tie the whole proceedings down to earth. He is one's guide to the labyrinth. For him, there may be punchlines, but there are no final answers: we live in the world *we* imagine, there's no eternal or transcendent Author.

The Lawyer's tale ('Speculation in Lost Causes') digresses along similar lines when he remembers asking, as a child, the hopeful question, 'Father, what is poetic justice?' and sets unravelling a splendid nonsense-string of associations:

> '... rapnuckle for rape, rosemary for rue, Roland for Oliver, holocaust for hankypanky, Sodom and Gomorrah for pinochle, two Macbeths for a Duncan, for tit three tats ...'

The narrative patterns are often extremely finely worked, with stories within stories and repeating motifs, but there are nearly always loose ends. Sometimes one gets no 'plot' at all, but a study or vignette: 'In Doulcemer' is an especially (nastily) effective example of this type, about an artists' colony that has replaced a dying peasant community with its own moribund 'uprooted, homeless, casteless' style of life. 'In Doulcemer' is a study in gossip, the verbal miasma given off by twentieth-century decadence (the stuff of so much literary biography). But even much more traditional material takes on a conscious, ambivalent air. 'Gaspard' (the Frenchwoman's story) goes back to eighteenth-century France for a saga of tragic adultery that's heavy with 'folk' feeling, yet it's so studiedly 'innocent' that it, too, feels somehow equivocal and overripe. The Frenchwoman herself suggests that it's like a tapestry – 'embroidered vines . . . village tales whose tissues long ago fell in tatters in the sun' – and it's a metaphor that applies to many of the other pieces too, with their focus on texture and detail, and their lurking snaky threads of narrative gold.

There are other reasons why this metaphor seems particularly apt. For one thing, it mingles and confounds 'art' with 'craft' in a way that would obviously appeal to Stead, since it spreads the privileges (and the burden) of creativity much more widely than conventional distinctions allow. One of the recurrent themes of the *Tales* is the question of individual 'genius', of originality, and the myths that surround those prestigious notions. The Centenarist is (as usual) a sceptic: it is, he argues, 'a matter of chance whether real talent is chosen or trampled under in the mud', 'much great talent is buried in arts and pursuits which are not considered elegant'; and, conversely, that there is no 'unmistakable hallmark of personality' that marks out every line or note or smudge by a 'man of genius'. As the others remark, he produces if anything too many arguments – especially for someone in his line of business (though he is unabashed: 'I sell best-sellers'). Nonetheless, he rouses the Mathematician to a fury ('the Centenarist is denying my individual soul') which produces one of the most suggestive and frightening of the *Tales*, 'The Mirror'. In it, the ability of mirrors to 'reproduce' the image of the self is slyly confused with procreation (children as 'reflections' of their parents) to produce a domestic nightmare. The story's tragic heroine Griselda is assailed from two directions at once – from the dead past (the old man she childishly imagines living in the mirror, an apish spectre) and from the future embodied in her children – and though she shakes off the first threat, the second is ineluctable; her body tells her (in dreams of unbearable vividness) that new life means decay, that the myth of individual integrity can't withstand the general urge-to-live:

> She saw . . . the surface of the germinating earth: horribly suggestive roots and cotyledons arose waving violently and tossing their sensitive blinded tips as if in the grip of primitive and ruthless passions . . .

This is 'creativity' as a force that grows through people. Her son is in league with the old spook in the mirror, reflections drown her. The Mathematician, it seems, has refuted his conviction, his 'individual soul' in venturing into the story's hall of mirrors.

Which is – or seems to be – Stead's own sense of the deepest message of the form, the dark implication hiding in its endless possibilities. Her 1968 essay 'Ocean of Story' talks of 'the million drops of water that are the looking-glasses of all our lives': the story (like the mirror) at once reflects us, feeds our sense of difference and diversity, and at the same time submerges us. In this sense, all talent is 'buried', a drop in the ocean as it were. It's a daunting and heartening creed –

> Any treasury of story is a residue of the past and a record of the day . . . Some may and will die; but man's story never.

So everybody, on her logic, 'has a bit of artist in him' and every artist contains multitudes. Speaking to Joan Lidoff in 1973, she put it very directly:

> . . . another fatal idea that belongs to the bourgeoisie, that

there's something sacred inside which if you dig out it will make you an original. And again it's a silly idea. There's nothing inside. It must be developed first. Well, there's something inside, but what? It's an amoeba, or something like that . . .

That 'amoeba' is Christina Stead's special fingerprint, the distinguishing mark of her mind and sensibility. Ironically enough, of course – since it's also a reminder of what she saw as the protean pond life we all come out of.

Small wonder *The Salzburg Tales* received respectful but rather wary reviews back in 1934: it's a book that attacks the cherished notion of the artist set apart, in the very act of celebrating creativity. When you come down to it, what she's implying is that there's plenty for everyone ('How can anyone store up this vast natural treasury?'), a most subversive suggestion, then as now.

VI

DJUNA BARNES

Nightwood

Some portraits of the artist are so dramatic and satisfying that they make writing a plausible Life absurdly difficult. In the case of Djuna Barnes, there was no one culprit who fixed the image, she seemed cut out for the part. Her fatal singularity, her beauty and her style have made her a kind of expatriate 1920s mascot – all the more so since she combined the roles of sex-object and predator, author and 'character'. Witty, bisexual, savage, self-immolating, Barnes presents a problem of definition precisely because she is excessively defined already. Look at her lipstick sneer, the perfect turn of her slim ankle. As a statement, she's grotesquely succinct. 'One cannot live on bird cries and cat calls,' she famously said. Which fits the picture.

Phillip Herring admits he faces a problem: 'When she left [Paris], the best part of her life was over. The name Djuna Barnes is synonymous with Paris café life in the 1920s, which she brought to life in *Nightwood*.' His own prose – the way the word 'life' keeps repeating itself – signals a certain weariness at this point, though he has managed to get to page 156 before putting a name to his difficulty. That *Nightwood* (1936) is a famously obscure book doesn't help, either, for its freakish images exude glamour, like darkness visible. Barnes knew what was happening to her reputation in the long, long years she lived on in bad-tempered sickness and solitude in Greenwich Village: 'My talent is my character, my character my talent, and both an estrangement,' she wrote in 1963. (She still had almost twenty years to go: she died at ninety in 1982.) But talent wasn't the worst of it; she had – many people thought – a special genius for alienation. T. S. Eliot, in fact, drafting a tactless and subsequently suppressed book-jacket blurb for her late poetic play *The Antiphon*, wrote, 'never has so much genius been combined with so little talent'. She was compared with Emily Brontë by several people, including (when she was drunk) herself – and comparisons with Emily Brontë are notoriously a code for metaphysical misfits, exceptions, heroines of visionary excess. Antonia White wasn't being at all kind when she mused that 'Djuna has genius if anyone I know has genius'. (Barnes reciprocated: 'Keep on writing,' she wrote to White. 'It's a woman's only hope, except for lace-making.') A Life of Barnes must embark on some demystification if it's to have any substance.

Yet if she's not Bohemia's queen of the night, Djuna Barnes is at the very least one of those people whose lives are more 'made up' than most. After *Nightwood*, she took to inhabiting the book's version of Paris: 'I haunt the Place St Sulpice now, because I've made it in my book into my life ... I love what I have invented as much as that which fate gave me – a great danger for the writer, perhaps ...' By 'danger', she probably meant at the time the rather fey but dizzying prospect of blurring the boundaries of reality and illusion, modernist *trompe l'oeil*. More prosaically, what happened was that she co-operated in travestying herself, turning up in books like Robert McAlmon's *Being Geniuses Together*. Genius on this definition was indeed about possessing a certain quality of 'being'; producing real work was entirely another matter. Some did, some didn't. Barnes did, though her *oeuvre* isn't large. Gradually, as her life gets to be told more fully and straightforwardly, it may even be that our appreciation of that achievement will grow.

We start with what 'fate' (that is, family) doled out. It tells you something about her background that her outlandish name was the one she started life with in 1892 at the family farm in Cornwall-on-Hudson, and that her birth was not registered. Her indigent father Wald was a very *fin-de-siècle* patriarch, also something of a 'genius': he espoused free love, spiritualism and art. Perhaps name-wise Djuna got off lightly – her siblings were called Thurn, Muriel, Zendon, Saxon, Duane, Buan and Shangar, born more or less synchronously of two mothers, Djuna's mother Elizabeth (to whom Wald was married) and Fanny (to whom he was not). In 1912, for complicated, partly financial reasons, Wald divorced Elizabeth to marry Fanny, and Elizabeth and her children had to leave the shared 'Noah's Ark' of a house her money had helped pay for. The whole desperate mess was overseen by the person who'd brought Wald and Elizabeth and Fanny together in the first place, his mother Zadel. She had polished her Boston-bohemian style in good company, having (during her second marriage, and a spell in London in the 1880s, accompanied by curly-haired Wald) been a friend of Lady Wilde and Eleanor Marx. Zadel was a prolific poet, short-story writer and journalist and wrote for W. T. Stead's *Pall Mall Gazette* while she was in London. She was also a suffrage and temperance campaigner, a medium, and a great believer in free love – and it was she who persuaded Wald he was a visionary, and charmed his women and children into submission.

Her granddaughter Djuna shared her bed as a girl, and was treated to ribald letters when she was away from home, featuring cuddles and breasts and doubtful jokes. In this household, sex was everywhere, and it's hard (as Phillip Herring in his biography, *Djuna*, says) to decide what really happened – though it seems certain that in Djuna's adolescence Wald, that bullying prophet of love, forced her into an initiation (probably better described as a rape) at the hands of a nameless neighbour, and vicariously much enjoyed it. Then, before she was eighteen, Wald and Zadel persuaded her into a brief and doomed 'marriage' with the middle-aged brother of Wald's number two wife Fanny. Perhaps the divorce that split up this cosy commune was after all a blessing in disguise. At any rate, once away from Wald in New York, Djuna found her feet, and her voice, attending art school for a brief six months – 'Individual, strong, full of promise', said her school report, 'hard to convince' – and finding work as a journalist.

Father Wald's baby-farm put her off motherhood for life. In this she oddly resembles another problematic, rather younger woman modernist, Christina Stead, author of that murderous family saga, *The Man Who Loved Children*. Stead's father, like Barnes's, went in for cranky, inverted puritanism about sex and breeding, and both talked intimate play-languages with the children. This is Wald, to 21-year-old Djuna: 'You say that you are *in love* – but that was always more or less khronik with youse wasn't it? male or female this time? And who's the lucky dog (or dogess?).' He signed himself 'Your Operapa'. Barnes's whole style, you could say, was aimed against Wald. The West, for example, brought her out in an ecstasy of revulsion – 'it personifies everything in my father that I hated – Mark Twain – Bret Harte – Walt Whitman sort of thing – Ezra Pound and his hick-prune-chewing prose.' Forced into family life as Kay Boyle's house-guest, she complained bitterly: 'The bloody fecundity of Kay is revolting. She should have been a rabbit and written in lettuce.' And of course her main spokesperson in *Nightwood*, 'Dr' O'Connor, is an abortionist. She gives him the immortal line – 'I love nature as well as anyone, things all growing quietly and getting used up and dying and saying nothing, that's why I eat salad . . .' She would write about the city, and about people. Her cities are built of people. John Holms, Peggy Guggenheim's sometime lover, called her talent Chaucerian – 'nothing but people'.

In New York, she gravitated to Greenwich Village and the Provincetown Players, and her journalism specialised in fashions and freaks and puppets and stunts – an impeccably perverse agenda. For one piece, she had herself force-fed to find out what the suffragettes were going through. And she had a love-affair with a German-American, 'Putzi' Hanfstaengl, which foundered disastrously during the First World War, when he decided he wanted to have German babies to compensate for the carnage. (Putzi later became a member of Hitler's entourage, and Barnes nearly landed an interview in the early 1930s using him as a contact, but Hitler proved too pricey; too pricey for Putzi too, who changed sides back, in 1937.) Posted to Paris (1921), she lived in the city of the ex-pats within the city: 'your love for Paris is a romantic passion,' her perceptive friend and fan Emily Coleman told her sternly: 'little to do with Paris's reality . . . you don't feel pressed upon in Paris because you are not in the least aware of French life that is going on around you'. It was for her a brilliant and productive decade, in which she flirted with the high-toned lesbian set that surrounded Nathalie Barney, mocked with warm malice in *Ladies Almanack* in 1928, and – the same year – published a first, autobiographical novel, *Ryder*. But this was easy meat. Her real life in Paris from these years was centred on her love affair with the sculptor Thelma Wood, from St Louis. Thelma mirrored her back to herself, in all her promiscuity and excess, and she suffered agonies of jealous pain in the process.

This was the stuff of *Nightwood*, the Paris of abject carnival, a kind of human menagerie. Those who wander this city want, impossibly, to *be* what they desire. Barnes's mouthpiece O'Connor is a Tiresias-figure, lipsticked and painted and blue-chinned, Robin/Thelma is lost to drink and other lovers, Nora/Djuna listens for her in the night as though she is listening to her own heart, with shame and fury: 'Robin is incest, too.' Willa Muir, years later, described the book's effect very well: 'You have entered into every kind of human distortion . . . you have a genius for imaginative empathy, and that is why your language wells up with a force that is relatively primitive . . .' Entering into her characters, she kidnapped them on to the page. Nathalie Barney told her Thelma was suicidal, having contemplated her metamorphosis. O'Connor's original, Dan Mahoney, turned on her with fury, as she recounted in a terrified but also somehow gratified letter. He hit her and cursed her, 'Then he vomited – & in the end flung himself on me asking if I "loved him", or at least respected him!! I don't know how I had the courage to say no.' She'd gone to Mahoney for an abortion in the early 1930s, after Thelma and she had parted for good, when she was involved in a series of affairs of no lasting significance. The real business of those years was writing it all up.

One of the most interesting parts of Herring's narrative, in fact, is the story, not of *Nightwood*'s inception, but of how it ever saw the light of day, how it was written, rewritten and wrenched into publishable shape. From this angle, as Cheryl J. Plumb's edition amply confirms, the figures most important to the book weren't the originals of its grotesque characters, but Barnes's patrons, friends and – in the case of Emily Coleman – self-appointed critic, editor and agent. The main patron was Peggy Guggenheim, for it was at Hayford Hall, the English West Country house she rented in the summers of 1932 and

1933, that Barnes did much of the writing; and it was there she met Coleman – clever, obsessive, the best sort of literary groupie (she'd recently been employed helping anarchist Emma Goldman with her memoirs). Coleman wasn't a lover of Barnes, but a lover of her work, and it was she who pushed her to organise and condense her chaotic material, in the absence of the props offered by normal 'novel' conventions. Barnes was perfectly aware, thanks to rejections from a host of publishers, that she wasn't a proper novelist, in any sense; 'they all say that it is not a novel; that there is no continuity of life in it, only high spots and poetry – that I do not give anyone an idea of what the persons wore, ate or how they opened and closed doors, how they earned a living . . .' It was Coleman who injected the (extra-textual) realism, acted as the go-between with the prosaic practical world, enabling her to keep and even intensify the book's poetic qualities. She seems to have more or less blackmailed Barnes into producing the book – 'To have someone love my book so much is a terrible responsibility,' wrote Barnes. 'Hitherto I had nobody to live up to but myself, now I have you.' As Plumb says, 'what the record shows is that Coleman's intense excitement over the human truths of *Nightwood* helped keep Barnes focused on the work, willing to rewrite'. And next, of course, Coleman badgered T. S. Eliot into wanting to publish it. Plumb, again, shows that his contribution, and cuts, though he 'blurred sexual, particularly homosexual, references and a few points that put religion in an unsavoury light', were not particularly significant. Plumb's text, taken from the typescript of the first edition, with copious apparatus, restores them, but doesn't change the character of the text very much in the process.

The moral seems to be – as we knew from biographies of Joyce and Lawrence and others – that great modernist works eat up lives. In Barnes's case, this was especially obvious, both because of the way she used the stuff of her own intimate life, and because of the vital role Emily Coleman particularly played in getting the show on the road. On the first score, Barnes reflected, 'the writer is a bastard ... for at least out of his miseries he makes a book'. Mahoney, that horrible night, had told her enviously, 'he could not understand how I'd become a legend on *nothing* – that I was a déclassé bitch with lesbian friends no better'. Getting the act together was the great, extra, unfair thing. And she nearly didn't, as this Life makes clear, not on her own. The title, though, was hers, not, as is sometimes said, Eliot's. Her greatest difficulty was that the very intimacy of her material inhibited her: 'the innermost secret ... should only be exposed in art ... when it is done for money, it becomes (for me) a brothel of the spirit.' Emily Coleman rescued her from this guilt. She had, of course, her own agenda – she read the book as a kind of metaphysical guide to salvation (later she would convert and become a proselytizing Catholic), but she had no designs on Djuna in life. She conducted a perfectly separate and very busy bed-hopping career of her own. Interested as she may have been in immortality, the kind she produced for Barnes was strictly literary, as she foresaw it would be: 'People you have never heard of and would ... never talk to, dreadful intellectuals, and Bloomsbury potentates, passionate lovers of literature, seers and prophets, will be among your audience.'

To find such a complementary spirit was against all the odds. The book nearly didn't happen, less because of the mystery of Art, than for lack of dialogue with the world. After it was published in 1936, Barnes sold her Paris flat (1937), and took herself shortly afterwards back to Greenwich Village. She broke her long years of silence only when, Phillip Herring says, she was driven to give up drink, in order to take revenge on her family for sending her to a sanatorium: 'When she realised that only sober and only with her pen could she pay off old scores, she turned her attention away from the bottle and toward her family.' The result was *The Antiphon*, the only significant work of her later years. She stayed sick, intransigent, alone. She ate, and opened and closed doors every day, but that wasn't the kind of thing she had ever been able to write about, after all. Herring says, with tact, that 'She required bitterness as the fuel of her art, and in that sense posterity owes some gratitude to the Barnes family (and Thelma Wood) for making Djuna Barnes angry enough to produce her finest work.' It's hard to disagree – except that one should add Emma Coleman too. Her work was all about loneliness, but it wasn't produced in isolation.

VII

VIOLET TREFUSIS

Hunt the Slipper

Hunt the Slipper, published in 1937, was Violet Trefusis's fifth novel, though only the second she had written in English. In fact it's a splendidly malicious commentary on England, and on the aristocratic English culture that she'd escaped (and been expelled by) eighteen years before. Englishness is lovingly anatomised from her adopted French — or as she liked to claim, with some justice, 'European' — point of view. Philistinism reigned still, she was unsurprised to see, and prudery. Her surviving English friends, she noted a few years later during her reluctant wartime retreat to her native shores, wouldn't like her any less if she didn't write: '(for some it would be, if anything, a relief).' To English tastes, wit — as opposed to humour — was a dubious, alien development. Like one of her characters, middle-aged Molly in the opening pages of *Hunt the Slipper*, they feared the 'chilly symmetry' of Paris, yearned for the 'motherly gloom' of London; they dreaded continental dinner parties: 'Here was no indiscriminate laughter to mantle the halting phrase; instead . . . silence, polite and expectant. One was never sure whether one had said something idiotic or not.' The authorial tone is deliberately, teasingly, cool and 'alien'.

However, Violet Trefusis was equally conscious that she hadn't escaped, hadn't really got away with it, and it's this wry awareness that makes *Hunt the Slipper* one of her best books. While she mocks insularity (not for nothing does she start with

Molly engaged in a bit of cosy topiary) she mocks too at the preoccupations that have, for her, replaced England, Home and Beauty – the addiction to travel (Violet was, like one of her earlier fictional heroines, 'une debauchée géographique'); her passion for her country house ('Ambush' in the novel borrows its anthropomorphised menaces and charms from her tower of St Loup, outside Paris); and her rapacious appetite for *bibelots* and possessions. Her character Molly Benson may be 'Nordic, humorous, loyal, inelastic', condemned to type, but Molly's brother Nigel, that attractive and 'feminine' man who takes after their French grandmother, is no less ironically conceived. In his love-affair with youth and freedom, in the person of his neighbour's wife, passionate and intransigent Caroline, his author explores the elusiveness of the grand gesture, the awesome power of places and things to collect the people who think they collect them. By the time she wrote *Hunt the Slipper* she herself had become, as it were, collected – a chatelaine, a skilled and successful hostess, not at all the bohemian free spirit she'd once imagined. Hence the novel's vividness and edge: she mocked, but she colluded.

It's something of a shock to read her fiction after reading about her. You don't expect her self-awareness, because she has existed, especially since her death in 1972, largely as a picturesque figure of scandal and camp tragicomedy – the wild, spoilt and dangerous lover of his mother Vita Sackville-West in Nigel Nicolson's *Portrait of a Marriage* (1973); the (again spoilt, but this time discreet) companion of the fashionably Proustian and enormously wealthy Princesse de Polignac, metamorphosing by gradual stages (including carefully-chosen male lovers) into a full-blown and absurdly snobbish cosmopolitan eccentric, a sad travesty of her passionately nonconformist youth. (*Violet Trefusis, Life and Letters* by Philippe Jullian and John Phillips,

124

1976; *A Solitary Woman* by Henrietta Sharpe, 1981.) The story of her life (outrageous-woman-into-'character') seems to consign her to the category of the written-about. However, she doesn't merely belong there: she salvaged her own perspective on the social and sexual mêlée, and on the strategies by which one survived. Her writing is of the sort usually called 'brittle' and 'clever' – English terms of disparagement that operate, rather like the distrust of 'wit', to register the 'other', the foreign. The light malicious tone is, of course, a by-product of her relative rootlessness, her distractions and limitations (as Henrietta Sharpe points out, she never had to work, and all too often didn't), but it's also an ironic recognition of her spectacular failure to reinvent the world.

She'd begun, years before, as Muse. When her own first novel was published (*Sortie de secours*, in 1929, when she was thirty-five) she'd already played this embarrassing role in works by two others writers: as 'Eve' in Vita Sackville-West's *Challenge* (written in collaboration with Violet at the height of their love in 1918–19), and as 'Sasha' in Virginia Woolf's *Orlando* (1928), where she's the Muse at one remove, seen through Woolf's own obsession with Vita. Reading *Challenge* now (finally published in England in 1973; it was withdrawn before publication in the 1920s, though it did appear in America in 1924) you glimpse Violet as an improbably hectic *fin de siècle* inhabitant of the novel's fictional Greek island republic, as eternally feminine as the name Eve suggests. Each time she enters, it's with a snaky train of duplicitous epithets: 'difficult, intractable, exasperating, subtle, incomprehensible'; 'spoilt, exquisite, witty, mettlesome, elusive, tantalising'; 'unaccountable, passionate, embarrassing'. Vita casts herself as cousin Julian (male, straightforward, preoccupied with the responsibilities of the governing class) who is at once betrayed and inspired by Eve. Eve is an anarchist, and she threatens (you might say, untying the allegory, which is fairly transparent anyway) the *safe*, private freedom Vita has found in her marriage to Harold Nicolson (each free to go his/her own sexual way) – threatens too Vita's relationship with her sons, her house, her money, her public image. Violet/Eve wants Vita/Julian to give up playing the aristocrat/matriarch and join her in her world of permanent exile:

> ... a new world – Eve's world, ephemerally and clandestinely populated. He contemplated it in fascination, acknowledging that here was an additional, a separate art, insistent for recognition, dominating, imperative ...

This is the invisible kingdom of the grand pariahs: 'the poet, the creator, the woman, the mystic, the man skirting the fringes of death – were they kin with one another and free of some realm unknown?' *Challenge* returns a dusty answer to this question. Eve can't leave her mental island after she's jealously destroyed the public 'cover' of their illicit love, and wilfully (and conveniently) drowns.

Violet didn't, of course. But she did challenge Vita, in letter after letter, to live up to the vagrant, gypsy gene she'd supposedly inherited from her Spanish grandmother. Some of the fictional Eve's most high-flown and sibylline sayings are matched pretty exactly by Violet to Vita – 'You *owe* yourself to the world of art, the world of colour, of adventure, of enterprise, of hazard, of free love' (1919). There are more laboured, and more convincing appeals too:

> Don't you see ... that if you tried for a hundred years to make, say a Fijian, see things from your point of view, you would never succeed. And your trying to make me see

is just as futile. I shall just go on playing my solitary games until you will listen to my point of view, which, in reality, is neither selfish nor immoral, but just DIFFERENT. (7 May 1920)

Or again, getting closer to home, and to the themes of *Hunt the Slipper*:

> It's all nonsense: one doesn't really need tapestries and carpets and pictures.
> This is what one needs: the person one loves, the sun, freedom ... My instinct is to crave for beauty in all its divers manifestations. I mean indoor — not outdoor — beauty. And I am ruthlessly repressing it, *because it isn't essential* ... You see, darling, wanting beautiful things really means wanting money ... I want passionately to be hardworking and free ... (5 June 1920)

Her failure to enter the world of living, starving art as Vita's sole and scandalously acknowledged Muse had driven her to momentary furious resolutions on her own account — 'I will write the most mad, obscene, relentless book that ever startled the world' (12 June 1919) — but her most frequent tone was despairing: 'I write to you in the most homeless, friendless, condition it is possible for anyone to be in. All morning I have been making lists of my things' (10 July 1920). 'Things' were, as she'd for some time suspected, the answer. Why not, since they constituted so much of the problem in the first place?

It was this consciously pathetic insight ('no-one who loves me and lives with me, no possessions, no reputation, no hope, nothing' (18 March 1921)) that led her to patch up her own hopeless marriage to Denys Trefusis (so far a grotesque failure as 'protective colouring'), to start life again in Paris, and – eventually – to write. Not the 'mad, obscene, relentless book', but surprisingly neat studies of desire displaced on to 'things'. Her characters are very seldom allowed even pets. It must be clear, as in *Hunt the Slipper*, that they relate to *objects*: 'Funny', writes Caroline to Nigel, 'I should have fallen a prey to two collectors.' And it *is* 'funny' – comic because it's so routinely perverse. 'Don't start making an inventory, it's always a bad sign,' says sensible Molly. It doesn't do to contemplate the fabric of one's existence too directly: something uncollectable may be missing. Violet, in her own idiosyncratic fashion, is here picking up an obsessive motif of late Victorian and Edwardian fiction. Sir Anthony Crome, for instance, Caroline's frigidly correct husband, recalls Meredith's egoist Sir Willoughby Patterne, or even James's Osmond in *Portrait of a Lady*. He's altogether a smaller, sillier and sadder figure, but he shares their deadly capacity to translate art and sexuality into the stuff of lists, objects ordered and paid for (preferably, of course, by previous generations).

Less optimistic than her predecessors, Violet toyed nastily at moments with the notion that the acquisitive mania was, possibly, the essential Eros. In her fragmentary and discreet autobiography *Don't Look Round* (1952) she wrote:

> It is not an exaggeration to say that places have played at least as important a part in my life as people. Indeed it is almost as though the places had generated the people . . . Vita belonged to Knole, to the courtyards, gables, galleries; to the prancing sculptured leopards, to the traditions, rites and splendours.

She makes no mention of their love-affair, nor of their abortive elopement, but in a way what she's saying here is just as shocking as that would have been. The one-time Muse ('You *know* we're different – Gypsies in a world of "landed gentry"') has adopted the values of the world she hated, but satirically, and immoderately, and with a vengeance. People are figures in the tapestry of their family backgrounds: houses and furniture give birth to them, lend them their sex appeal ... Virginia Woolf's fantasy-celebration of Vita in *Orlando* must have struck Violet as a splendid illustration of this perverse principle. As she follows Vita/Orlando through the centuries, Woolf shows her accruing value and complexity and androgynous charm; whereas the Violet-character, Sasha, makes a brief, comet-like appearance as a Russian princess, fleeting, alien, French-speaking:

> English was too frank, too candid, too honeyed a speech for Sasha. For in all she said, however open she seemed and voluptuous, there was something hidden; in all she did, however daring, there was something concealed ... she never shone with the steady beam of an English woman ...

Again Violet is cast as the dangerous, duplicitous Muse. She, however, I'm suggesting, came to see the people who live in and through things (including herself) as more truly perverse.

In her French novel *Broderie anglaise* (1935) she works this through with elegance, wit and some bitterness. Alexa, a middle-class intellectual (Oxford professor's daughter and novelist and a little like Virginia Woolf), is entangled in a tormenting affair with the aristocratic Lord Shorne (who has something of Vita about him, including a teasing touch of foreign ancestry from his Neapolitan mother). His charm is inextricable from his 'place'; he has an inherited ease with the whole world of objects: 'she discovered that sensuality didn't lie, as she'd thought, in some single, special gesture. Sensuality could be present in everything, in the way one lit a cigarette, or peeled an apple.' The scene of her seduction in a state bedroom is marvellously funny. As the candles are lit, objects come forward to take their bows – 'The silver console with the arms of Charles II? Present. The Mortlake tapestry of Joseph undressing for the embraces of Potiphar's wife? Present . . .' Against her better judgement, Alexa is smitten. And Violet allows herself a brief authorial disquisition: you must never forget the extraordinary prestige the aristocracy enjoy in the minds of the English middle class – 'Snobbery is the main motive force in English life.' John, Lord Shorne, is of course a sham, a hollow man. He's told Alexa that he can't commit himself to her because the great love of his life, his cousin Anne, betrayed him, but she discovers when she meets this *femme fatale* (who is, of course, rather like Violet) that it was John who couldn't go through with their marriage, because he's the creature of sterile habit, of his background, of his formidable mother (who rather resembles Vita's mother, Lady Sackville).

Broderie auglaise, besides neatly turning the tables on *Orlando*, reveals the link between one major theme in Violet's fiction – Eros versus possessions – and another: the dominance of the matriarchal principle. It's often said of women writers that their male characters are really women; in Violet's case, except when they are, like Sir Anthony in *Hunt the Slipper*, almost entirely sexless, it's taken for granted. They're 'front men', as it were, for some formidable woman (usually mother) in the background. You might suppose that, given her sexual preference for women, Violet was merely doing what she pleased here, but no. The matriarchs in her fiction enshrine all the values (places, possessions, propriety) that deny her heroines their desires. The matriarchs defuse and diffuse sexuality, making their sons spiritually impotent and – much more unforgivably for Violet – their daughters too. Thus, in *Hunt the Slipper*, both Nigel and Molly Benson are in different ways trapped by their love for their dead mother; Nigel's feminine (though not effeminate) nature is his major charm, but his disastrous inability to leave the past and his possessions behind is the other side of the same coin.

This is why, though he loves Caroline expertly, he'll never love her absolutely, never leave his world for hers. She is Violet's most vital heroine: clever and beautiful, of course, but also teasing, piquant and (necessarily) ruthless. She's a 'gypsy', with a natural distrust of possessions, and, like the Violet of twenty years before, she's a fanatic in love. While she may enjoy beautiful things and trivial things too (nightclubs, parties) she's ready to sacrifice all for truth and passion. She is appalled by the ease with which she and Nigel can live a double life (Sir Anthony being at once too arrogant and too sexless to notice) and wants to divorce, to run, to force the world to see: 'she had longed for risk, exposure, privation, a hardening of the muscles'. She echoes Violet's plea in her letters to Vita – 'I wish we had to work, work hard' – and Nigel, like Vita, fails to take up her challenge. For the fate that rules the plot is matriarchal, all comes back to mother. As, probably, for Violet it did. Her own mother, Alice Keppel, was at least as important a bar to her passionate adventure with Vita as Vita's own (matriarchal) values and *her* mother. It was Mrs Keppel who pushed on her marriage to Denys Trefusis, and who engineered the failure of her attempt to run. Not, so far as one can gather, out of any particular horror of Violet's sexual proclivities, but out of instinctive respect for the proprieties and the social fabric. But Mrs Keppel – mistress of Edward VII, shrewd, sensual, brilliantly acquisitive, tough, lavishly and universally charming – is too large-scale a personage to deal with here. If one's not careful she'll billow in, as she did so often in Violet's life, and make her daughter's unhappiness, obliquity and dissatisfaction seem unreal compared with her confident and decorous hedonism. She resembled, wrote Violet in *Don't Look Round*, 'a Christmas tree laden with presents for everyone'.

She does not, in any case, put in direct appearances in the English fiction. One glimpses her perhaps in the Baronne de Petitpas in *Les Causes perdues* (1941), a woman devoted to the cult of happiness: ' "Only happiness is aesthetic," she was in the habit of saying.' When her protégée Marie-Charlotte announces that her marriage is an empty parody, Mme de Petitpas is momentarily stumped, but soon recovers herself: 'still you'll be able to entertain' –

> *To entertain* . . . you'd have sworn that doors opened, that a glittering crowd thronged down a staircase out of Tiepolo; that musicians tuned their instruments, while liveried flunkies bowed to the very ground . . .

Mrs Keppel's real importance to Violet's fiction, however, lies in the fact that the world it portrays is the kind of world she enjoyed, a world her daughter failed to reinvent, but inhabited in an ironic and parodic spirit. The game, in *Hunt the Slipper*, is fixed in advance, Violet is, by now, as much in complicity with pusillanimous Nigel as with passionate Caroline. 'She had none of the frivolity of the older generation,' she remarks coolly of her heroine – 'Latent in her mind was the theory that the world was well lost for love's sake.' The older generation's frivolity has patently triumphed in the Violet who wrote those lines. It had been all along her curious fate to foresee her future: 'you'll only play at being free and bohemian,' she wrote savagely in

1919 to Vita, who planned to go to Paris not with her, but *en famille* with Harold: 'You will talk art and poetry; people will say witty, brilliant things, a man called, I think, Jean Cocteau, notably . . .' Which is more-or-less exactly what happened to Violet herself, along with the houses and possessions and the role of hostess.

Like her heroine Caroline she'd once thought of herself as a 'changeling' (no one really knew who her father was, except that it was neither Mr Keppel nor Edward VII): in her old age she hinted at royal blood and put on grotesque pretenderish airs. She several times staged, in her fiction, lurid scenes in which loveless old ladies make inventories of their jewels, and play at changing their wills – and, sure enough, she went on to act it out herself. 'From social rebel,' says her biographer Henrietta Sharpe sadly, '. . . to embodiment of those simulated virtues.' However, as I've tried to suggest, there's rather more to it than that. Violet parodied the values she was immured in. Her cosmopolitan progress (more gaudy and odd as years went by) exaggerated and mocked the social prowess of women like her mother. There is always with her a sense of distance, of alienation, of incipient absurdity, of mimicry almost, though that is to put it too strongly. Really it's a matter of the subtler ironies of conscious bad faith, of residual scepticism. *Hunt the Slipper*, like all the best of her writing (*Broderie anglaise*, *Les Causes perdues*, *Don't Look Round*), fascinates because of its lucid recognition of the unfreedom that lurks in the heart of extraordinary privilege. The great amorous or artistic adventure eluded her, but she made memorably stylish comedy out of her defeat.

VIII

JANE BOWLES

Two Serious Ladies

There were originally three serious ladies, but the story of the third – Senorita Córdoba – was never finished. From the passages about her that survive, however, you can tell that she was as wonderfully unpredictable as Miss Goering and Mrs Copperfield:

> The traveller and Senorita Córdoba were seated together having a chat.
> 'Doesn't love interest you?' the traveller was asking her ... 'Deep down in your heart, don't you always hope the right man will come along some day?'
> 'No ... no ... no ... Do you?' she said absent-mindedly.
> 'Who, me? No.'
> 'No?'
> She was the most preoccupied woman he had ever spoken with.

One source of the comedy of Jane Bowles's serious ladies is their anarchic, deadpan style. They never take other people's natures for granted. After all, their own impulses are mysterious to them. Nothing is natural, anything is possible. The Senorita makes this American traveller in Guatemala look like a mere tourist. Soon he'll be packing his case, 'with the vivacity of one who is in the habit of making little excursions away from the charmed fold to return almost immediately'. Serious ladies, by contrast, embark on their perverse adventures without return tickets. Senorita Córdoba, like other Bowles characters, is probably bisexual, and prefers women – but that is only the beginning of the story.

The book was written in the late 1930s and early 1940s and published in 1943, and parts were inspired by Jane's honeymoon trip to Central America with her husband, Paul. They married in 1938, the day before her twenty-first birthday, and although both chose same-sex sex it wasn't at all merely a marriage of disguise or convenience. They would often live apart, but they always kept in close touch, and only her death divorced them. They proved well suited – they were card-carrying members of the American avant-garde and (briefly) of the Communist Party, and even lived for a short while in the famously queer household at 7 Middagh Street in Brooklyn Heights, where W. H. Auden made the house-rules and queenly striptease artiste Gypsy Rose Lee had written *The G-String Murders*. It was in 1940–41 that the Bowleses took over Gypsy Rose Lee's rooms; from 1947 they lived on and off in Morocco, mostly in Tangier. Wherever they lived, Paul seemed more at home than Jane. She envied and sometimes teased him for being such a well-adjusted misfit, and once declared to him that 'Men are all on the outside, not interesting. They have no mystery. Women are profound and mysterious – and obscene.' As Millicent Dillon showed in her excellent biography *A Little Original Sin*, Jane made a kind of private mystery religion out of her fascination with women's hidden lives.

Her character Christina Goering (named after Jesus Christ and Hitler's aviation minister) as a girl invents a grotesque ceremony in which she subjects her sister's meek best friend Mary to a mock-baptism – 'If you don't lie down in the mud and let me pack the mud over you and then wash you in the stream, you'll be forever condemned.' Mary is duly dirtied and drenched, but emerges no more mystically one with Christina than she was before:

'The three minutes are over, I believe,' said Christina. 'Come darling, now you can stand up.'

'Let's run to the house,' said Mary. 'I'm freezing to death.'

Sensible Mary doesn't die or undergo a conversion, all that happens is that Christina is confirmed in the loneliness of her calling.

In her adult life the same 'promptings' lead Miss Goering first to adopt at random various ungrateful and unattractive hangers-on, and then (to their disappointment and indignation) to sell the comfortable house she has inherited and renounce middle-class life: 'I really believe that it is necessary for me to live in some more tawdry place . . .' Taking her entourage with her, she settles in a cramped four-room house on an island not far from the city, which she has chosen for its squalor – 'one can smell the glue factories'. Once there, she takes the ferry to a godforsaken town on the mainland, where she continues to search out her destiny in encounters with strangers in a gloomy bar. Miss Goering disinherits herself, in short, and becomes an adventuress, and a serious lady. That is, a woman who turns her true character into an open question. Perhaps the most bizarre thing about Bowles's women is that the object of their quests is to lose themselves, to fall, to find glory in the mud.

They may seem to belong in the company of decadents enchanted by the glamour of the gutter. Traditionally, poetical prostitution *à la Baudelaire* had symbolised the hell-tinged happiness of hitting bottom. Bowles's serious ladies are certainly drawn to poverty, and they are warmed by the idea of prostitution. But the working girls she writes about are almost never imagined as abject or sublime, instead they have volatile moods, are often gay, and improvise moment to moment in a quite practical fashion. Mrs Copperfield, the second serious lady, on her own separate adventure in Panama, where she rents a room in the same sleazy hotel as her new-found friend, the prostitute Pacifica, whispers to herself: '. . . what an angel a happy moment is – and how nice not to have to struggle too much for inner peace! . . . No one among my friends speaks any longer of character – and what interests us most, certainly, is finding out what we are like.' Mrs Copperfield is in love with Pacifica's life, and wants to share it. Miss Goering is obscurely flattered when a 'big man in an overcoat' who is some sort of gangster picks her up. Like Senorita Córdoba and the traveller, Miss Goering and 'the heavy-setman who owned the hearse-like car' engage in one of those crossed-purpose conversations between straight men and dubious women that Bowles finds so hilarious:

'Well,' he said to her after they had been sitting there for
a little while, 'do you work here?'
'Where?' said Miss Goering.
'Here, in this town.'
'No,' said Miss Goering.
'Well, then, do you work in another town?'
'No, I don't work.'
'Yes, you do. You don't have to try to fool me, because
no one ever has.'
'I don't understand.'
'You work as a prostitute, after a fashion, don't you?'

Miss Goering laughed. 'Heavens!' she said. 'I certainly never thought I looked like a prostitute merely because I had red hair; perhaps like a derelict or an escaped lunatic, but never a prostitute!'

True to her promptings, however, she decides to play along with his mistake. Sexual relations with men will never be 'profound and mysterious', but being taken for a prostitute will put you in touch, perhaps, with a world of women that is endlessly strange.

The serious ladies want to live outside themselves. And that is a want they share with their author, who is herself the third, invisible, serious lady of the book. Like them, Jane Bowles had fled the prospect of a respectable middle-class life. She was born in New York in 1917, the only child of second-generation immigrants, a Jewish-Hungarian mother and a German-Jewish father, Claire and Sidney Auer. They lived on Long Island, but Jane returned to the city with her possessive and ambitious mother when her father died in 1930. She'd had a limp as a child, and after a riding accident in her teens developed tuberculosis in her knee-joint; she spent 1932–4 having treatment in a Swiss clinic, and in 1936, back in New York, the leg was fixed so that it would never bend. This didn't cramp her style – rather, it confirmed it. In moods of raucous defiance she'd call herself 'Crippie, the Kike Dyke'. Already in 1936, still in her plaster cast, she was keeping louche company in Greenwich Village bars and being deplored by her mother and her aunts. She reported to a crony, another middle-class drop-out and would-be writer, George McMillan, an emergency family conference: 'they all sat down and said . . . that I was a grand normal girl and that this Lesbian business was just an adolescent phase . . . and that if only I didn't have such an analytic mind I certainly would throw it off – and if I really were a Lesbian they'd get up a fund for me and send me down to the village in my own private bus . . .'

In fact, her travels, and her love-affairs, seem to have been driven by a desire for release not only from her parents' world, but from an American-Bohemian counterculture that too much resembled a little excursion from the charmed fold. Years after she wrote *Two Serious Ladies*, her quest culminated in Tangier, in her pursuit of the elusive Arab market-women Tetum and Cherifa. She wrote about this in a notebook with uncharacteristic and sad directness:

> I don't know which one I like best, or how long I can go on this way, at the point of expectation, yet knowing at the same time that it is all hopeless. Does it matter? It is more the coming home to them that I want than it is they themselves. But I do want them to belong to me, which is of course impossible . . .
>
> If I have broken through my own prison – then at the same time I have necessarily lost what was my place of rest . . .

Here the wit of *Two Serious Ladies* has deserted her. In the early 1950s Bowles discovered saintly, self-destructive Simone Weil's book *Waiting on God*, and found in it a mirror of her own sense of apartness. 'There are some human beings', Weil wrote, '. . . separated from ordinary folk by their natural purity of soul. As for me, on the contrary . . . I have the germ of all possible crimes . . . within me . . . It is the sign of a vocation, the vocation to remain in a certain sense anonymous.' We should aspire, she said, 'To empty ourselves of our false divinity, to deny ourselves, to give up being the centre of the world in imagination, to discern that all points in the world are equally centres . . .'

Weil believed in a deity outside the world, though whether He was the Jewish or the Christian God was never quite clear, and took imaginative refuge in the beauty of nature. Bowles by contrast portrayed the natural world as alien and uncanny. In *Two Serious Ladies* Mrs Copperfield takes a trip with her husband to a deserted beach in Panama:

> She watched him picking his way among the tiny stones, his arms held out for balance like a tight-rope walker's, and wished that she were able to join him because she was so fond of him . . . She threw her head back and closed her eyes, hoping that perhaps she might become exalted enough to run down and join her husband. But the wind did not blow quite hard enough, and behind her closed eyes she saw Pacifica and Mrs Quill standing outside the Hotel de las Palmas.

For Bowles, other people – other women – were the only hope of salvation (Pacifica will lead Mrs Copperfield into the water, and for once the blasphemous baptism will work). Perhaps art could save, too – but Bowles found it harder and harder to write, and her experiments in living were fraught with tension. She did set up house with Cherifa in Tangier, but it certainly wasn't a 'place of rest', since although liaisons between Western men like her husband Paul and Arab men were relatively accepted, even traditional, homosexual relations across the two cultures between women were entirely outside the rules, off the map. Such was the stormy atmosphere of scandal Cherifa and Jane generated that when Jane suffered a stroke, Tangier expatriate gossip speculated that Cherifa had poisoned her (though some said it was with a love potion). But even in the later years when, thanks to illness and obsession, the daily details of living absorbed more and more of her energy, there were frequent flashes of mirth. In 1958, for instance, the Beat poet Allen Ginsberg called Paul in Tangier, and got Jane instead – 'Then this complete madman asked me if I believed in God. "Do you believe in God, Jane?" I told him: "I'm certainly not going to discuss it on the telephone."'

So singular was Bowles's sensibility, and so exiguous her output – only the play *In the Summer House* and a handful of stories apart from *Two Serious Ladies* – that it's always been tempting to see her as one of a kind, writing in isolation when she did write. But the work does have precedents. Not in the soulful lesbian tradition associated with Radclyffe Hall (a red herring), but in the polished, modernist, mocking-and-despairing line of Katherine Mansfield, Djuna Barnes and the young Jean Rhys, who are all drawn to freaks and outlaws. When Ford Madox Ford wrote in his Preface to Rhys's first collection of stories *The Left Bank* (1927) of her profound knowledge of 'many of the Left Banks of the world', and her 'bias of . . . sympathy with . . . lawbreakers', he was describing this *demi-mondaine* heritage. Djuna Barnes's wise-cracking, elliptical newspaper interviews from the century's teens and twenties, featuring stars of burlesque, rabble-rousing preachers and dubious politicians, hit the same note. Here she is talking with actress Helen Westley, a member of the Washington Square Players, in 1917:

'. . . I say, go to life, study life. Sit on a sidewalk and contemplate the sewer, the billposters, the street-cleaners, the pedestrians, anything – but go there before you go to Chinatown to buy embroidery.'

'Do you often sit on the sidewalk, Miss Westley?'

'I do. If doctors would prescribe sidewalks instead of

pills and hot water, how much better off we should be.'

'Really, you have a dirt complex, as Freud would say.'

Barnes's modernist mistresspiece *Nightwood* (1936), inspired by the expatriate Parisian underworld, featured a narrative procession of freakish 'originals' – one of whom, Mademoiselle Basquette, 'a girl without legs' ('She used to wheel herself through the Pyrenees on a board'), seems to have inspired the grotesque story of Belle, who hasn't any arms either, and has been left behind by the circus, in *Two Serious Ladies*. It is Andy, another of the outsiders Miss Goering meets in the bar, who tells her about Belle: 'I began to notice her mouth. It was like a rose petal or a heart or some kind of a little shell. It was really beautiful. Then right away I started to wonder what she would be like; the rest of her, you understand – without any legs ... It grew and grew, this terrible curiosity ...' The stigma of deformity is for these writers, doubtless, a way of exploring their own estrangement as authors – even from the world of the male avant-garde. At the same time it reflects their defiant conviction that the writer's vocation is a marvellous act, a performance brought off against the odds.

Closest to Bowles in her own generation was Southerner Carson McCullers. They were born in the same year, and their careers had an eerily similar shape – almost all their real work done in their twenties, followed by years of writer's block, excesses and devastating illness, and early death. Both loved women and shared friends and fans among gay men, particularly Truman Capote and Tennessee Williams. In the McCullers bestsellers, *The Heart is a Lonely Hunter* (1940) and *The Ballad of the Sad Café* (1943), the grotesque is the order of the day. In a 1940 *Vogue* article, titled 'Look Homeward, Americans', McCullers wrote:

> We are torn between a nostalgia for the familiar and an urge for the foreign and strange. As often as not, we are homesick most for the places we have never known.
>
> All men are lonely. But sometimes it seems to me that we Americans are the loneliest of all ... Our literature is stamped with a quality of longing and unrest, and our writers have been great wanderers ...
>
> So we must turn inward. This singular emotion, the nostalgia that has been so much a part of our national character, must be converted to good use ... We must make a new declaration of independence, a spiritual rather than a political one this time ...

This is close to the ethos of Bowles's writing, and yet its sentimental and elegiac tone, the very ease with which McCullers can say 'we', marks a parting of their ways. Writing to Paul in 1947, Jane mulled over the difference: 'Certainly Carson McCullers is as *talented* as Sartre or Simone de Beauvoir, but she is not a serious writer. I am serious but I am isolated and my experience is probably of no interest at this point to anyone.' In the same letter she goes on to draw a distinction between herself and Paul, too. He may also be 'isolated', but his loneliness is somehow representative, unlike hers:

> Not only is your isolation a positive and true one but when you do write from it you immediately receive recognition because what you write is in a true relation to yourself which is always recognizable to the world outside. With

me who knows? When you are capable only of a serious
and ponderous approach to writing as I am . . .

She attached a special, semi-private meaning to the word
'serious'. For her, being serious meant risking the possibility
that you were meaninglessly weird, an existential Calamity Jane
– 'my kind of isolation I think is an accident and not inevitable'.
It also, however, meant writing with panache, hilarity and
devastating insight on the very edge of that particular abyss.
McCullers could say, 'When I write about a thief, I become
one.' It's hard to imagine Bowles feeling so readily identified
with her characters: when she writes about pariahs she only
partly reclaims them for the imaginable world. She said in this
same glum, stock-taking letter, 'I realize now . . . that really
"Two Serious Ladies" never *was* a novel . . .' She was right,
but in fact its improbability was its genius. With it she joined
the small company of women modernists who celebrated their
freakishness in the highest style.

IX

SIMONE DE BEAUVOIR

The Second Sex

Art is not a mirage

'Through literature', Simone de Beauvoir wrote, 'one justifies the world by creating it anew, in the purity of the imaginary, and by the same token, one justifies one's own existence.'[1] It may sound at this distance in time a safely vague, uplifting declaration of faith, but it was not. Indeed, she meant it as a kind of parody of other people's religions of art. Writing affirms human liberty, for Beauvoir, but only writing that has sloughed off the bad faith of sublimity and split religion. In this essay I want to look again at Beauvoir the writer as an iconoclast and a utopian. She has been mistaken for a realist, in part because of her open hostility to self-reflexive, experimental writing, but in fact she is, I shall argue, best understood as an anti-realist – a writer who systematically destabilised the relations between past and present, work and world, on which realism depends. She has more in common with the *nouveau roman*, and a novelist like Nathalie Sarraute, than might at first appear. She too is preoccupied with the writer's role – though in her case this leads her into autobiography, sexual politics and the obsessive demolition of cultural fictions. Her main creation was herself-as-writer: writing became for her a process of retreating ahead of herself, living for the future.

In *When Things of the Spirit Come First* (her early sequence of apprentice 'tales' eventually published forty years on, in

1979) she is savagely knowing at the expense of pretentious Chantal, who writes a diary designed to bear witness to her superior sensibility. An example: Chantal describes her search for lodgings in a provincial city where she's about to take up a teaching job:

> ... after I had looked at five dreary places ... I found this old house, whose massive outer doors seemed less to bar the entrance to a dwelling than the way into a soul. An exceedingly distinguished white-haired lady led me very graciously through the garden, and then through her apartment; even before I had seen my room I was entirely won over. These walls contain all that is most touching in provincial France: the mellow surface of the old furniture, the books in their rare bindings ... in every corner of this house the vanished past has left an impalpable scent – one that gives the present the rare and heady bouquet of a very old wine ... I feel more ardently than ever, that in spite of everything Life is wonderful.[2]

She is making herself imaginatively at home, snuggling down into a nest of stock responses which if she were English would have been woven out of Dickensian echoes, but in France suggest Balzac, with several generations of quotation in between. Chantal, in fact, has a taste for the modern – Proust, Rilke, Katherine Mansfield – but she contrives to turn everything she reads into a script for day-dreaming. She's well insulated against the raw real.

Chantal lies to herself as well as to others (this is her diary, after all), and she does it in the name of something ineffable she calls 'Life' – which is, of course, emphatically not what Beauvoir means by 'existence' ('one justifies one's own existence'). Looking back on the time when she wrote these stories, Beauvoir said that Chantal (though based mainly on a hated colleague) bore a resemblance to her own young self: 'If the bad habits which I attributed to Chantal irked me so much, that was because . . . I had slipped into them myself.'[3] Like Chantal, she says, she'd embellished her own life history, too, in those days. And she believed in 'Life' back then: 'Sartre and I were seeking some kind of "salvation" . . . we were, in fact, a couple of mystics. Sartre had an unqualified faith in Beauty, which he treated as inseparable from Art; while I attached supreme importance to Life' (*The Prime of Life*). Literature had to free itself from those nostalgic fakes, those dead Ideas or essences (Beauty, Art, Life) if it was to become a real vocation, a proper project.

The last story in *Things of the Spirit* was, Beauvoir said, the best (though she did not think she was saying much). It is certainly the nearest to a portrait of the artist, and it stages at the end a kind of anti-revelation. The world around the narrator, Marguerite, is stripped of its 'bouquet', and hence its bad magic: 'it was as though a spell were fading. Suddenly, instead of symbolic scenery, I saw around me a host of objects that seemed to exist in their own right. All along the pavement little cafés came into being . . .' This is the public world (Chantal nestles indoors), the world where you look on, write (all her life Beauvoir would write at café tables), share the space. Interestingly enough, Beauvoir privileges this character with a retrospective view of herself. Marguerite judges that her awakening may sound all too epiphanic: 'At the time I attributed too much importance to what I may call this kind of revelation; it was not a conversion of a spiritual nature that could rid me of spirituality . . . all I have wished to do was to show how I was brought to try to look things straight in the face, without accepting oracles or ready-made values.' At this point she ceases in effect to be a character at all, and merges with her author – recognisably the same writer who will say in her 1979 Preface, at seventy, 'In the end, her eyes are opened, she tosses mysteries, mirages and myths overboard and looks the world in the face . . .' You trade in Life for the world, the old cosy writing that lent significance and soul to things for a new world of existence, where people and things are on a level, the realm of what she and Sartre called contingency.

So writing begins with a process of demystification. The early stories, clumsy as they were, mapped out many of Beauvoir's abiding themes, and even some of her later strategies. The quest for a point of vantage on one's self is the same one that will inspire her to write the story of herself as a writer in the autobiographies; and the obligation 'to try to look things straight in the face' stays with her to the bitter end. She became the kind of writer she was because she feared fictions ('mysteries, mirages and myths'), and she feared them because she saw them not as securely separate from the way people lived their lives, but as interwoven with our whole understanding of ourselves as characters. If she put real people into her novels, that was because she habitually assumed that people lived in and with fictions. In other words, the boundary between books and the world was permeable: 'To write a novel', she wrote in 1966, 'is somehow to destroy the real world.'[4] Her whole life's work, and *The Second Sex* in particular, depends on the conviction that people are constructs: we come from the matrix of the culture at large, not from God, or nature, or (even) Mother.

If Beauvoir had found a publisher for *Things of the Spirit* in the late 1930s, it would have been part of the same literary moment as Sartre's novel *Nausea* (1938) and Nathalie Sarraute's first book, her collection of cunningly unclassifiable short fictions,

Tropisms (1939). In the event the war put iconoclasm on hold, in any case. But it is worth reflecting on the common ground they shared, which was not yet the site of *literary* war between the self-consciousness of the *nouveau roman* and existentialist 'commitment'. Until the great falling-out in the 1950s it was enough that (as Beauvoir said) Sarraute 'was hostile to all essentialism' (*Force of Circumstance*). Her attacks on mystery and false consciousness were very recognisable – though she was from the start a much more fastidious and consistent craftswoman than Beauvoir. One of her favourite tricks was to dive under the surface patina of the 'real' to discover the way it is processed and pre-digested for us. Witness this description of a chorus of bourgeois ladies at work in a teashop, from Tropism X:

> '... he won't marry her. What he needs is a good housewife; he does not realise it himself. Certainly not; I mean it. What he needs is a good housewife ... Housewife ... Housewife ...' They had always heard it said, they knew it: the sentiments, love, life, these were their domain ...
>
> And they talked and talked ... continually rolling between their fingers this unsatisfactory, mean substance that they had extracted from their lives (what they called 'life', their domain), kneading it, pulling it, rolling it until it ceased to form anything between their fingers but a little pile, a little grey pellet.[5]

This is how essences are 'born', over and over again. Beauvoir in *The Second Sex*, in her marvellously bleak chapter on 'Women's Situation and Character', says: 'it is not matter she comes to grips with, but Life, and Life cannot be mastered through the use of tools, one can only submit to its secret laws. The world does not seem to woman "an assemblage of implements" intermediate between her will and her goals, as Heidegger defines it.' She goes on to remark that pregnancy and cooking teach woman a fatal patience: 'time has for her no element of novelty'. Repetition is *of the essence*: it is how essences reproduce themselves.

In making this connection between Beauvoir and Sarraute I am trying to place Beauvoir not merely as an enemy of mystification, but also as an anti-realist. She may invoke 'objects', 'matter', 'things' and 'existence' as writing's proper material, but that makes her as much a sceptic about *classic* realism as Sarraute. Novels in the great nineteenth-century tradition, with their elaborate strategies for creating perspective, continuity and typicality, and finding the universal in the particular, depend on precisely the kind of metaphysical or magical underpinning Beauvoir wanted to demolish. Compare Roland Barthes (the very early Barthes, who in 1953 sounds still rather existentialist) on the nineteenth-century novel: 'the true is supposed to contain a germ of the universal, or to put it differently, an essence capable of fecundating by mere reproduction, several orders of things among which some differ by their remoteness and some by their fictional character'.[7] In her hands, fictional narratives veered back towards earlier eighteenth-century and Enlightenment modes of mimicry, and first persons jostled third persons on the page. As Sarraute said in her brilliant 1950 essay 'The Age of Suspicion', the distinctive sign of contemporaneity was the way writers and readers had drawn closer together. The writer's urgency to make it new – to unmake convention – became the more-or-less openly admitted theme of the narratives of now. For Beauvoir, pursuing the author's vocation became itself a vocation. She lacked the subtlety and skill and sheer passion for (and against) words of Sarraute. She was in love with the idea not of making something (the *nouveau roman* was a problematic literary object, shot through with auto-destructive irony, yet it was clearly obsessively crafted) but of self-invention, 'transcendence'. So when she broke the rules of the traditional novel form – as she did in her two most ambitious fictions, *She Came to Stay* (1943) and *The Mandarins* (1954) – it was not in order to make the *novel* new, but in order to say something about the role of the writer. In the first, she committed a barefaced authorial murder that was in no sense in her character's character: 'by releasing Françoise through the agency of a crime . . . I regained my personal autonomy', she said in the autobiography (*The Prime of Life*); anything was preferable to having her *alter ego* submit to being 'just a woman'. In *The Mandarins* she gives the authorial role to (third person) Henri, and allows her (first person) heroine Anne nowhere to speak from, and no access to writing. As Susan Rubin Suleiman points out, in an interesting essay on Beauvoir's writing self, the narrative structure is anomalous: 'Anne's narrative discourse is impossible . . . Here, then, is a curious chiasmus: Anne who is the subject of enunciation, neither speaks her narrative, nor writes it.'[7] Beauvoir readily sacrifices formal logic and decorum in order to make her escape from her own novels, in short.

Transcendence she describes in *The Second Sex* as 'escape towards some objective, through enterprise'. The world of transcendence is wide open, has a 'sky'; whereas the girl growing up discovers that society does not want her to become 'an autonomous and transcendent subject': 'The sphere to which she belongs is everywhere enclosed, limited, dominated, by the male universe . . . there will always be a ceiling over her head, walls that will block her way.'

This metaphorically housebound woman is so thoroughly domesticated by the culture that she can – like Chantal –

believe herself emancipated, a free spirit. She is, perhaps, never more self-deceived than when she sees herself as having a special intimacy with poetry, and with nature: 'Poetry is supposed to catch what exists beyond the prose of everyday; and woman is an eminently poetic reality since man projects into her all that he does not resolve to be.' All sorts of 'spiritual hocus-pocus' (*The Prime of Life*) are generated in the attempt to disguise this state of affairs, and from time to time in *The Second Sex* Beauvoir tries on the 'line', in a spirit of gross mockery: 'Society enslaves Nature; but Nature dominates it. The Spirit flames out beyond Life; but it ceases to burn when Life no longer supports it. Woman is justified by this equivocation in finding more verity in a garden than in a city, in a malady than in an idea, in a birth than in a revolution.' Women carry ideas, they are in fact conscripted by the culture at large (by men, that is) as signs and exchanged like messages (this was famously pointed out by Lévi-Strauss),[8] and when they use signs themselves, they often do so bad faith, without a real vocation: 'for the vast majority of women an art, a profession, is only a means: in practising it they are not engaged in genuine projects'. Women read as if they were playing solitaire, and write or paint without disturbing the stereotypes that shape their lives. No wonder Beauvoir so distrusted not only traditional forms of fiction, but any pursuit of art that seemed (as of course avant-garde experiments like Sarraute's did) to cultivate a *mystery*.

The archetypal non-project, though, is 'embodying' meanings. Women are regularly endowed with allegorical significance, they are vessels or containers for abstract ideas. Or perhaps one should say, as Beauvoir does, that mythic Woman does this kind of higher housework: 'She is the soul of the house, of the family, of the home. And she is the soul of such larger groups, also, as the city, state and nation ... in ...

statues that represent France, Rome and Germania ... the Church, the Synagogue, the Republic, Humanity are women; so also are Peace, War, Liberty, the Revolution, Victory ...' But still, and always, she is inside a 'house' built of fictions. Liberty may be a woman, woman incarnates the 'mystic mana' of (say) Democracy, while women are unfree, unrepresented. This is the territory Marina Warner explored in *Monuments and Maidens* in 1985, with – appropriately enough – a chapter on the public statuary of Paris, a city particularly rich in stone sirens and civic saints.

Stone is the right stuff, because it emphasises the way woman is construed as timeless – that is, exiled from history. Myth turns you to stone, 'the Eternal Feminine, unique and changeless'. And yet, of course, there is nothing actually fixed about woman's meaning: she can and does embody quite opposed symbolic values, she is a wandering signifier – 'woman incarnates no stable concept'. Beauvoir reels off whole lists of woman's allegorical roles: 'Renown and glory are women; and Mallarmé said: "The crowd is a woman".' And she develops her own distinctive brand of mock-modernist poetry as she celebrates woman's wonderful versatility – 'She is the triumph of victory ... she is the vertigo of ruin ... There is a whole world of significance which exists only through woman ... she is the source and origin of all man's reflection on his existence.' The most important words in such sentences are not the grand nouns like victory or ruin (which are mini-allegories, fictions, false constants), but the verb to be, and the flat-sounding 'existence'. Woman *is*, man reflects on his *existence*: woman is ontologically compromised, she 'is' in bad faith. But what about that 'is' in the last sentence – 'she is the source ... of all man's reflection' – is that a false construction too? Certainly it is a compromised 'is', since it relates, not to a quality of being, but a state of affairs, a situation that we can change; it is inessential. Beauvoir, as her commentators have noted, does sometimes make essentialist oppositions sound terminally true, as if she forgets, or loses faith in, her theoretical confidence that women are in fact part of history's processes. For now, however, I want to point to her overriding, destructive euphoria. If you want access to the present and the future, you find it in the (anti-)art of demystification – 'it is by denying Woman that we can help women to assume the status of human beings'.

It is not, then, excessively paradoxical to argue that *The Second Sex* comes closer to fulfilling literature's project, for Beauvoir – 'one justifies the world by creating it anew' – than her novels. Toril Moi is, I think, making a very similar point when she says that *The Second Sex* is 'the direct result of . . . her autobiographical impulse'.[9] Taking over from the patriarchal author-gods who exiled women from history, Beauvoir declares: 'I shall place woman in a world of values and give her behaviour a dimension of liberty. I believe that she has the power to choose between the assertion of her transcendence and her alienation as object. . . .' In other words, 'It is not nature that defines woman', but culture. Many of Beauvoir's most eloquent and memorable sentences make negative assertions of this kind: most famously the one that says one is not born a woman, but becomes a woman. Other examples: 'man is not a natural species: he is a historical idea'; 'one is not born a genius, one becomes a genius'; 'essence does not precede existence: in pure subjectivity, the human being *is not anything*'; (on lesbian relationships), 'Because they are not sanctioned by an institution or by custom . . . they are all the more sincere'; and, heroically and finally (though one could cull many more), 'There is no such thing as an "unnatural mother"'. The spirit of contradiction animates and inspires her prose whenever 'nature' threatens, or when nature's bourgeois apologists and their traditions are in question, particularly marriage and the family – 'The family is not a closed community . . . the couple is a social unit'. She will go out of her way, on odd occasions, to mock nice middle-class ladies by treating their domestic pieties as vices. Thus, we are told of a woman who 'took to orderly housekeeping as others take to drink'; and later on, describing women's confinement in various separate spheres she learnedly and maliciously alludes to 'a dull gynacceum' – which she glosses as 'brothel or middle-class home'.

In practice her solemn definitions of a literature that sides with change – 'Literature assumes sense and dignity when it makes its appeal to persons engaged in projects . . . integrated with the movement of human transcendence' – are realised in this eager iconoclasm, which is a form of utopian anti-art. It is perhaps worth remembering that in the autobiography she says that she liked 'hermetic poems, surrealist films, abstract art, illuminated manuscripts and ancient tapestries, African masks' and had 'a passion for watching puppet shows' (*The Prime of Life*). During her visit to the United States in 1947 she dined with Marcel Duchamp one evening, after lecturing at the New School in New York; and a party given in her honour was attended by Kurt Weill, Le Corbusier and Charlie Chaplin.[10] Her avant-garde credentials were in good order at the time she began work on *The Second Sex*. She was conscious, too, that although she was seen in the United States as a spokesperson for existentialism, her sex rendered her, still, an anomaly – 'an existentialist *woman* was more than they could tolerate' (*Letters to Sartre*). This, as it turned out, was to be the time when she 'chose herself' – when she decided that her American love-affair with Nelson Algren was not to change her life radically; when she returned to Paris, Sartre and the role of the New Woman;

and when she entered on middle age. She would note ironically that many a middle-aged woman 'suddenly undertakes to save her lost existence'. Hers had not been 'lost', of course. But it was only now that she justified herself, in her own terms, by uncreating mythical Woman.

Born, again

Woman she sees as impregnated with generality and timelessness: myth makes the 'real' woman, and in particular myth makes the mother. It is on the topic of motherhood that Beauvoir is most herself – that is, most radical, outrageous and inventive. Motherhood is the original of women's oppression, and of the many forms of mystical *mauvaise foi* with which they attempt to disguise it from themselves. It is woman's 'misfortune to have been biologically destined for the repetition of Life', she is in bondage to the species. It is on this note that the book begins and ends: 'It is her duty to assure the monotonous repetition of life in all its mindless factuality. It is natural for woman to repeat, to begin again without even inventing, for time to seem to her to go round and round without ever leading anywhere.' In fact, here, she is describing housework, not childbearing, but you can see how the language picks up on *repetition*. When she says 'it is natural', here, she means that women's character follows from their situation, which seems (but only seems) to assimilate individual lives to a general pattern. (Her distrust of realism in its nineteenth-century form finds weighty confirmation here, too. Realist representations looked at from her angle, are a way of reproducing the world as it is, adding to its plausibility and seeming finality.) Mother is the mythic being – the false universal – that upholds the binary oppositions that oppress actual women: immanence/transcendence, essence/existence, natural/historical, and so on. And since myths are not safely locked away in books, but work in and through our lives, then mother is a menace. You have to give birth to yourself, become self-made, and make mother redundant, in order to *exist*.

So her chapter on 'The Mother' starts, logically enough, with abortion. The gothic brutality of the gesture is still shocking: or perhaps it would be truer to say that it has become shocking in a different way from the one Beauvoir had in mind. She was intent on demystifying and secularising maternity, in a Roman Catholic culture that outlawed not only abortion but contraception. She wanted to separate sex-for-pleasure and reproduction. All of which now seems too obvious for words, but is not, by any means. Feminism itself has encouraged a certain amnesia on this issue, by making new myths of motherhood, as if the old, bad magic had been safely exorcised. As Elaine Marks says, Beauvoir's line on motherhood made her suspect in her turn to a younger generation: 'The most famous French women theorists of the past fifteen years – Hélène Cixous, Luce Irigaray, and Julia Kristeva – have been adding to the sacred untouchable quality of the figure of the mother within our patriarchal Judeo-Christian tradition . . . in their search for a feminine specificity, they have once again magnified mother and motherhood.'[11] Marks could have found matriarchal attitudes closer to home, too, of course, notably in the work of Adrienne Rich. Since Marks's essay was published in 1986 gender studies have developed in directions that make more sense of Beauvoir again – towards notions of (gay) self-fashioning, and a critique of ahistorical or nostalgic views of the sexual character. The self-creation of transsexuals, the discussions of the politics of fertility that surround test-tube babies, surrogate motherhood, cloning and male 'pregnancy', all underline the fact that the human body, and particularly the woman's body, is less a secret garden than a public thoroughfare scrawled over with slogans.

Not that younger feminist writers all found Beauvoir's demystificatory savagery alienating. Fiction writers in particular – so many of them now un-writers, or re-writers – sympathised with her strategies. Angela Carter, in her 1977 novel *The Passion of New Eve*, and her polemical anatomy of powerlessness, *The Sadeian Woman* (1979), was very much in the Beauvoir tradition: 'The nature of actual modes of sexual intercourse is determined by historical changes in less intimate human relations, just as the actual nature of men and women is capable of infinite modulations as social structures change . . .'[12] Indeed, in ironically enlisting Sade as an ally Carter was realising a project Beauvoir only sketched in her 1953 essay titled 'Must We Burn Sade?'[13] Beauvoir's use of Montherlant in *The Second Sex* follows the same unscrupulous pattern: his attacks on motherhood would be fine, she says, if only he were not actually myth-making in his turn: 'If Montherlant had really deflated the myth of the eternal feminine, it would be in order to congratulate him on the achievement: it is by denying Woman that we can help women . . .' The affinities between Carter and Beauvoir are less obvious than they might be because Carter in her fiction adopted the old magical motifs and turned them on their heads carnival-style, rather than abusing and banishing them as did Beauvoir. Margaret Atwood, too, re-engages with the themes of *The Second Sex*. Her 1973 novel *Surfacing* was bewitched by exactly the mystique of motherhood Beauvoir attacked: 'The animals have no need for speech, why talk when you are a word. I lean against a tree I am a tree leaning . . . I am not an animal or a tree, I am the thing in which the trees and animals move and grow, I am a place.'[14] This nameless and pregnant narrator is an allegory of threatened Nature – in other words, very much the product of later twentieth-century culture, though neither she (nor her author) saw it that way at the time. Atwood produced her own revisionist treatment of the same myth (*as myth* this time) in her dystopian fable *The Handmaid's Tale* (1985). Her earlier fertility-fiction becomes a nightmare, set in a born-again biblical theocracy where women 'are' wombs – 'I sink down into my body as into a swamp, fenland.'[15] To be a place, a space, is to become, in this book, a carrier of the state's meanings. In Atwood's dystopia female literacy is being denied and abolished, women are words, they do not use them – or at least not in elaborate or public ways.

It is no accident that such revisionist writers home in on the Mother, and start to sound like Beauvoir. Woman in her role as Mother, *The Second Sex* argues, is symbolically gravid with timeless feminine wisdom, and so becomes deeply dangerous – 'the daughter is for the mother at once her double and another person . . . she saddles her child with her own destiny: a way of proudly laying claim to her own femininity and also a way of revenging herself for it'. And, as often, Beauvoir underlines her point about how exotic, perverse and disreputable bourgeois traditions are, by adding with an anthropologist's solemnity, 'The same process is to be found in pederasts, gamblers, drug addicts, in all who at once take pride in belonging to a certain confraternity and feel humiliated by the association.' Mothers hand on the habit, in short. Or as she puts it later, the child is 'already dreaming of Bluebeard and the holy martyrs'; or, again with a very straight face – 'The great danger which threatens the infant in our culture lies in the fact that the mother to whom it is confided in all its helplessness is almost always a discontented woman.' This is why the young women in Beauvoir's novels are almost hysterical with hatred for their mothers, or for anyone who represents the same kind of equivocal female authority, and – what is often even more puzzling – why the author lets them get away with a level of routine vileness of temper that seems out of proportion to any particular provocation they are offered. They are, it seems, inspired by an intuitive loathing of their elders' bad faith; and those elders, conscious of their guilt, quail before them. At such moments, even when the grown-ups (Françoise in *She Came to Stay*, or Anne in *The Mandarins*) are versions of Beauvoir herself, she sides with the 'daughter'.

Mothers give birth to their daughters twice over, in her world. The first, physical birth is relatively innocent, although pregnancy taints the mother with generality – 'in the mother-to-be the antithesis of subject and object cease to exist; she and the child with which she is swollen make up together an equivocal pair . . . Ensnared by nature the pregnant woman is plant and animal . . .' Women can salvage their sense of themselves as subjects, nonetheless. 'Mme de Staël', we're told briskly, 'carried on a pregnancy as readily as a conversation'. It is the second birth that traumatises both mother and daughter: that is, the shaping of the daughter into a woman, in the process of which mother becomes the medium for the wide world's cramping pressures. In Beauvoir's account she turns into a figure much resembling the wicked stepmother in fairy-tales:

Sometimes the child's gaiety, heedlessness, games, laugh-ter, are enough to exasperate her . . . why should her daughter, this other woman, enjoy advantages denied to her? . . . The older the child gets, the more does resentment gnaw at the mother's heart; each year brings her nearer her decline . . . it seems to the mother that she is robbed of this future which opens before her daughter . . . She keeps the girl in the house, watches her, tyrannizes over her . . .

The eerie feeling that we're in the land of fable is not inappropriate, since this is a *generic* role the mother is playing, not a particular person's part. An earlier passage spells this out even more clearly – 'the young bride . . . at her mother's side . . . seems no longer like an individual, but like a phase of a species . . . her individual and separate existence merges into universal life'. The mother is also rather like the bad fairy who lays a curse on the unfortunate princess – the curse of repetition, woman's 'nature', the big sleep in which she embodies 'the harmony of nature and society'. This is what incites all revolutionaries against the figure of the mother, says Beauvoir: 'in flouting her they reject the status quo it is intended to impose upon them . . .' To become a woman is to be programmed 'to conserve the world as given' in your turn.

And conversely, to make it new is to break the chain, by refusing to reproduce the world; to desecrate the shrines and expose the mysteries as conjuring tricks and old wives' tales. Beauvoir's sardonic eloquence in telling tales of mothers and daughters gives these passages a power she seldom musters when dealing with the same themes in her fiction, where she is at once less polemical and less inventive – though she does achieve similarly vivid effects by different means in the autobiographical writing. It is when she is smashing time-honoured icons that she feels her own separate identity as a writer most intensely. She may pile up enormous quantities of material in *The Second Sex*, but this has, formally speaking, the effect of oxymoron – vandalism-by-accretion – since the material is all there to demolish received wisdom. Or to put it another way: attacking the myth of motherhood, she has orphaned herself, cut herself off from the past. Now she is faced with the vertiginous prospect of writing for her life, authoring herself.

If a woman starts to see round the corners of the conventional picture – starts to let things slip deliberately out of perspective – the results are not going to be pleasant, even for a constitutional optimist like Beauvoir. Sartre in *Nausea* has his anti-hero Roquentin look in the mirror and see not a face but a meaningless puffy assemblage of colours and textures, a Frankenstein mask; and when he contemplates the ocean, his mental eye penetrates the glassy surface to the seething (pre-human, post-human) marine life underneath. The year before the publication of *The Second Sex* he had written a Preface to Nathalie Sarraute's first novel – *Portrait of a Man Unknown* (1948), a kind of anti-portrait of the artist – in which he congratulated her on her 'protoplasmic vision of our interior universe': 'roll away the stone of the commonplace and we find running discharges, slobbering, mucous, hesitant, amoeba-like movements . . . these viscous, live solutions'.[16] Sartre was doubtless recognising the language of 'sliminess' he had employed in *Being and Nothingness* to describe the 'in-itself' – 'It is a soft, yielding action, a moist and feminine sucking.'[17] Sarraute, as he says admiringly, has found a richer vocabulary for this new sub-textual stuff than he had. She describes 'inner' life – the life that is usually decently 'clothed' and contained in a realistically-described character – in skinless detail. Her narrator in *Portrait of a Man Unknown* much enjoys the ghoulish sport of picking people apart, looking inside their skins – 'to find the crack, the tiny crevice, the weak point as delicate as a baby's fontanelle . . . And all that remains of the firm, rosy, velvety flesh of these "live" persons is a shapeless grey covering from which all blood has been drained away'. This new life is a *decomposing* life, a life that does not – as the conventional picture does – deny the presence of death; this 'protoplasm' is a metaphor for the stuff of life we share with the things around us, grey matter that resists the projects of consciousness.

Beauvoir uses the same imagery in *The Second Sex*, and applies it to the bodily situation of women. Nonetheless it is important to recognise that this is a style of literary discourse – a discourse about the horror of the new (in both senses, the horror belonging to the new, the revulsion caused by it) generated out of deliberate efforts of defamiliarisation. So it is not merely a symptom of Beauvoir's personal psychopathology, nor a private, perverse language shared solely with Sartre. If you suspend the habit of seeing embryonic existence as Life, this is the prospect that opens before you:

> This quivering jelly which is elaborated in the womb (the womb, secret and sealed like the tomb) evokes too clearly the soft viscosity of carrion for [man] not to turn shuddering away. Wherever life is in the making – germination, fermentation – it arouses disgust because it is made only in being destroyed; the slimy embryo begins the cycle that is completed only in the putrefaction of death.

Like Sarraute (and Sartre) Beauvoir is producing a counter-myth about a levelling of material processes, eliding the distinctions between human and non-human, decomposing and composing.

Still, it is not clear in this passage how far she means us to see 'disgust' as a squeamish male reaction or as a *human* response to a contingent world that forces on us a sense of absurdity. The problem is even more pressing when one comes to a later and more famous passage about women and slime:

> Man 'gets stiff', but woman 'gets wet' . . . If the body leaks – as an ancient wall or a dead body may leak it seems to liquefy rather than to eject fluid: a horrid decomposition.
> Feminine sex desire is the soft throbbing of a mollusc . . .

woman lies in wait like the carnivorous plant, the bog, in which insects and children are swallowed up. She is absorption, suction, humus, pitch and glue, a passive influx, insinuating and viscous: thus, at least she vaguely feels herself to be. Hence it is that there is in her not only resistance to the subjugating intentions of the male, but also conflict within herself.

The question of *who she is speaking for*, so often unresolved, is here for once directly addressed – no doubt a measure of Beauvoir's embarrassment. It is woman who feels herself to 'be' this slimy, sucking bog, 'vaguely', graphic though the list is. This, however, does not really sort out the question of bad faith entirely, since it may well be that she only experiences herself this way as a result of internalising cultural propaganda. So we can, if we like, absolve Beauvoir of an essentialist picture of women's bodies as inessential and absurd. But perhaps there is not much point in the manoeuvre, since so far as 'feeling' goes ('thus . . . she vaguely feels herself to be'), this present-tense woman (whatever the future may hold) is self-divided, and contemplates her own genitals with fascinated horror. Indeed, most readers probably read 'I' for 'she', and take this passage as an example of what Beauvoir now feels 'free' to say, having ditched the reticence and mysticism with which women were conventionally supposed to veil their sexual parts from themselves.

The swamp imagery conjures up the surreal prospect of genitals with 'a life of their own' (also a presage of death). Sartre's Roquentin in *Nausea* had had a sea-food hallucination too, once his body stopped seeming to him like a tool. Beauvoir in the autobiography describes, from an amused distance in time, some mescalin-induced horrors he suffered, and which fed his depression, on turning thirty, at the idea of becoming 'a mere passive object' (*The Prime of Life*) – 'behind him, past the corner of his eye, swarmed crabs, polyps and grimacing Things'. The slime passage in *The Second Sex*, which is so riveting and awkward precisely because it is neither distanced nor 'owned' by Beauvoir, is followed, unsurprisingly perhaps, by twenty-odd pages of very uneven writing. There is a bad-tempered and chauvinist attack on the American practice of 'safe' sex before marriage (she probably means what was known as 'heavy petting'), which she thinks leaves girls technically deflowered but also uninitiated. Then, as if to prove her own credentials as a 'real' woman, she produces a praise of carnality which seems entirely to have forgotten the horrors (above) of mollusc moisture: 'True sexual maturity is to be found only in the woman who fully accepts carnality in sex desire and pleasure', who will be someone 'of ardent temperament' naturally, as opposed to those frigid Anglo-Saxons. This – not the horror-writing about slime – is the sort of thing that reveals Beauvoir at her most vulnerable to her own favourite charge of bad faith. But then again, a few more pages on, she is writing like a paid-up and conscious utopian:

> The erotic experience is one that most poignantly discloses to human beings the ambiguity of their condition; in it they are aware of themselves as flesh and spirit, as the other and as subject . . . the very difficulty of [woman's] position protects her against the traps into which the male readily falls . . . he hesitates to see himself fully as flesh. Woman lives her love in more genuine fashion.

The sense of ambiguity as (this time fairly certainly) *human* – as a situation to be lived and not a symptom – represents a significant move into different territory. Difference does not

171

mean, necessarily, a self/other (or true self/false self) divide, but multiplies and divides inside one's life.

Beauvoir and Sartre habitually talked of themselves as 'one'. Toril Moi goes so far as to say that 'the myth of the unity between herself and Sartre functions as one of the most fundamental elements in her own sense of identity . . . the one untouchable dogma of her life'.[18] I am not convinced – or not exactly. For Beauvoir this 'one' had continually to be invented. It was Sartre who, she says, encouraged her to use her own life as material for her writing. They are seated (where else?) at a café table in Paris at the end of the summer:

> 'Look,' he said with sudden vehemence, 'why don't you put *yourself* into your writing . . . ?' The blood flushed up in my cheeks; it was a hot day and as usual the place was full of smoke and noise. I felt as though someone had banged me hard on the head. To put my raw, undigested self into a book, to lose perspective, compromise myself – no, I couldn't do it, I found the whole idea terrifying . . . It seemed to me that from the moment I began to nourish literature with the stuff of my own personality, it would become something as serious as happiness or death. (*The Prime of Life*)

This was the moment writing became a real project, we are invited to infer; and the fruit of the decision to put herself ('raw, undigested') on to the page, *She Came to Stay*, 'embodied my future. I moved towards this goal with effortless speed . . .' (*The Prime of Life*). The imagery announces the inception of her first published book as if it were a brain-child – she is giving birth to herself. It is worth noting also, however, that the scene from the autobiography is itself embodying the process it talks about – living in public, a sort of communal creation, a running commentary on a writing life. I suggested above that it was in *The Second Sex*, rather than the novels, that she realised her project of originality most fully. Perhaps, however, it would be truer to say that it was in writing across the boundaries of genre that she found her *métier*, and that *The Second Sex* was the book that confirmed her in this sense of her vocation.

Elaine Marks, in the essay already quoted, has some very suggestive and apposite things to say about Beauvoir's interpretation of her role as a writer:

> Simone de Beauvoir has consistently broken with decorum and has written directly about those topics one does not write or speak about today except in the discourse of empirical social science, of jokes, or through metaphor. It could, therefore, be maintained that the originality of Simone de Beauvoir's discourse is precisely this act of trespassing. She has not obeyed the taboos placed by the institutionalization of specialized discourses on the body, sexuality, ageing, and God; she has not remained within the acceptable boundaries marked by level of style or genre that tell a reader this is a poetic text, a scientific text, a philosophical text.[19]

This negative originality – 'She has not obeyed ...' – creates an enhanced sense of *playing* the writer, living writing, not only producing books, but producing more writing about the earlier self that produced them ... This way one keeps one jump ahead of oneself; and one keeps, too, a privileged, ever-shifting point of view. Beauvoir lays her own experience on the line, ageing becomes her topic (for example) because she will not accept the indignity of inhabiting the ready-made character lying in wait for an old woman. And in her account of the decomposition and death of part of herself, in Sartre, she deconstructs the myth of the great man who's all mind.

Behind the scenes

Where in all this is transcendence? Beauvoir's eternal return to her own situation and character (the novels made of fictionalised fact, the autobiographies, the interviews, the private letters made public) starts to look oddly like the kind of sub-art she castigates. For example: give any discontented woman a chance, she says nastily, near the end of *The Second Sex*, and she'll turn into a fake artist or a pseudo-writer: 'Woman's situation inclines her to seek salvation in literature and art . . . With a little ambition, she will be found writing her memoirs, making her biography into a novel, breathing forth her feelings in poems.' Although Beauvoir had not yet written any memoirs, she had certainly turned a lurid episode from her biography into a first novel. The final mocking gesture above, about 'breathing forth . . . feelings', insulates her from this feminine art sunk in immanence and bad faith, of course, since she is entirely innocent of poetry. But why is she sailing so close to the wind here, almost daring herself and her reader to make the connection between her iconoclastic refusal to write decorously separate, invented fictions, and the self-expressive not-quite-fiction indulged in by middle-class women with time on their hands? Did she still think at this stage that she would write positively utopian, speculative fictions? Possibly, given that she had had a stab at it in *All Men are Mortal* in 1946. Or was she engaged, as I rather suspect, in the vertiginous game of revealing how very little ground there was on which to stand in *good* faith? In fact, it is almost as though good faith consists in doing the same things, but with the awareness of their provisionality, particularity and in-built irony.

As early as 1939, in a letter to Sartre, she produced what she referred to jokily as 'a whole dissertation on this privileged character one always accords to *oneself*'. It is a fascinating example of her thinking under pressure and on the run, and explains a good deal about the function, for her, of their oneness. The setting is the latest of their three-cornered intrigues:

> When you love someone trustingly ... you take each tender act, each word, not as *true* but rather as a signifying object: a given bit of reality with respect to which the question of truth isn't posed. By contrast, however, the tender acts or words of the said beloved person with a third party (let's say with Wanda) appear like constructed objects – they're 'bracketed off'. The difference is not that you think in one case: 'He's telling me the truth' and in the other: 'He's lying to her.' You may very well concede that he isn't lying to the other person, but truth itself is disarmed here, appearing almost a matter of luck – since it could be false. Whereas in your own case you do not even have that reflective idea of *truth* – the bracketing does not occur. This explains how far illusion can go ...

Without a metaphysical guarantee of Truth shorn of pure reference, the only way she can see of getting beyond fictions is in *dialogue*, an exchange of words that transcends words (Socrates would have agreed). She concludes, in the letter – absurdly and heroically – 'When I say we're as one ... it means we're beneath reflection.' This last phrase is a splendid way of describing how she manages to keep her future, real self out of the picture, out of the question. Sartre is her double, her witness, pooling perceptions and judgements with him she has a place to stand in utopia. So she can author her fate by retreating ahead of it.

Such an argument implies that bodily separateness, and gender difference, are themselves at some level fictions. To a whole generation of feminists this looked like nonsense. However, a more recent reader like Judith Butler readily makes sense of it: 'the body is a *field of interpretive possibilities*, the locus of a dialectical process of interpreting anew a historical set of interpretations which have become imprinted on the flesh'.[20] You can understand Beauvoir's insistence on the necessity for transcendence, Butler argues, if you understand gender as 'an active style of living one's body in the world'.[21] The body 'wears' our 'cultural history':[22] in other words, the body is eminently interpretable, and (conversely) consciousness is not the flesh. Beauvoir had acknowledged as much: 'The fact is that every human existence involves transcendence and immanence at the same time.' To say this is also to acknowledge that from now on we have to make up difference as we go along. For Butler this is of course a central tenet – one is freed, or doomed, to inhabit one's images and language 'performatively'. Having nowhere else to stand but at a temporary point in a whole series of interpretations has become second nature.[23] For Beauvoir, it was, I think, nearly always a bleak and reluctant adventure, though it was what made her know herself a writer and alive.

In old age, she said, woman often acquires willy-nilly an ironic, unillusioned gaze: 'she has seen in man not the image on public view but the contingent individual, the creature of circumstance, that each man in the absence of his peers shows himself to be'. This is a woman who has been behind the scenes. In the event, a quarter of a century on, it was Sartre who declined first, and whose body leaked and decomposed. Her report from behind the scenes of his last years, *Adieux* (1981), caused scandal by its references to the absurd indignities of age, and particularly his incontinence. In a sense, however, she was paying tribute to the notion of themselves they had so long sustained, as people who could face the worst without false consolations. She talks about the precautions taken to prevent journalists and photographers spying on his last, comatose hours in hospital, wanting not only to protect him, but to take charge of the horrible truth *herself*: 'I made as if to lie down beside him under the sheet. A nurse stopped me. "No. Take care . . . the gangrene." It was then that I understood the real nature of the bedsores. I lay on top of the sheet and I slept a little.'[24] In the same volume she published transcriptions of the taped conversations between the two of them that had taken the place of reading and writing for him as he grew blind. Some of his ruminations have a particular relevance to the project of transcending fictions: 'There's one thing I've always thought – I spoke about it to some extent in *Nausea* – and that is the idea that you don't have experience, that you don't grow older. The slow accumulation of events and experiences that gradually create a character is one of the myths of the late nineteenth century and of empiricism. I don't think it really exists' (*Adieux*). Beauvoir likewise was always wary of the narrative habits that make for reconciliation, and smuggle back into material lives a metaphysical notion of wholeness, a kind of afterlife spelling fulfilment.

So she remained an anti-realist. Her strategies as a writer were all to do with banishing the mellowing perspective and the soulful and structuring typicality of classic realist writing.

She reported, blow by blow, from the battlefront of her life, and the books were themselves part of the battle. So her encounters with literariness are not the kind that lead you 'on' into formal experimentation, but the kind that lead you 'back' into the character of authorship in our time. The fictions Beauvoir was interested in did not flourish solely between the covers of books, but in the culture at large, which continues – for example – to think of 'genius' as male (Beauvoir: 'One is not born a genius, one becomes a genius'), and mystify the (phallic) magic of making it new. Christine Brooke-Rose, after a long career as an experimental writer, and a lifetime's discreet silence on such matters, made the same points from a very different angle in her essay 'Illiterations': it was, she said wryly, almost as difficult as getting women into the priesthood, getting the right quality of attention for women's writing that invented new tricks.[25]

Beauvoir (as with Sarraute) would have been unsympathetic; would have thought that formal experimentation was a distraction from the real business of tracking down the lies that shape people's lives. She became very brisk about this towards the end of her own life. Her biographer Deirdre Bair reports a throwaway line on Virginia Woolf: 'Yes, Woolf is among the writers whose works I admire and sometimes reread, but only her feminist writings because I don't agree with her novels. They don't have any center. There isn't any thesis.'[26] Nonetheless, from her own very different angle, and from behind the scenes, she was converging on the same mental territory when she asked Sartre in their late conversations about how the old dichotomies of active/passive (and by implication masculine and feminine) applied to his experience of writing: 'as I work with my pen, and as I write', he replied, 'I have not really refused passivity . . . there is an element of passivity in my work' (*Adieux*). Indeed, one might argue that, as against received notions like 'The Death of the Author', Beauvoir's demystificatory exploration of the *life* of the author emerges with considerable credit for prescience as we survey a period in which biography and autobiography – and particularly literary biography and authors' autobiographies – have so proliferated.

Beauvoir wanted to think that the life of the writer was a representative life, that it stood for the project of self-choice and human freedom. But does the burgeoning of such 'lives' bear her out? Often it looks very much as though (auto)biography is the refuge for the comforting realist assumptions exiled for the most part from 'serious' fiction. Phyllis Rose, in her Introduction to *The Penguin Book of Women's Lives*, quotes a confession from a biography-addict, Kennedy Fraser: 'For several years in my early thirties, I would sit in my armchair reading books about these other lives ... I felt very lonely then, self-absorbed, shut off. I needed all this murmured chorus, this continuum of true-life stories to pull me through. They were like mothers and sisters to me . . .'[27] She would read 'furtively', she says, 'as if I were afraid that someone might look through the window and find me out'. Beauvoir would have been horrified, one imagines, to be hailed (as she is by Phyllis Rose) as one of these 'mothers of the literature of women's lives',[28] if what it meant was feeding the closeted, self-regarding character of the unreconciled-but-inactive woman, the woman insulted, the woman in bad faith. On the other hand, Kennedy Fraser, looking back on her sedentary self, knows very well what she was up to – she is looking in through that window, coolly, her eyes unsealed, a self-writer in something of the Beauvoir mould, though a good deal more amenable and forgiving.

In the end, it is Beauvoir's intransigence that is so impressive, for better and for worse. Instead of recanting when, reluctantly, sometime during the 1940s it seems, she accepted that putting *oneself* out of the picture – 'beneath reflection' – was indeed a mental conjuring trick, she proceeded, in *The Second Sex*, and the autobiographies, to invent the impossible, unillusioned ground on which to stand. Is this bad faith? It seems so heroical a version of it, if so, that it deserves another name. She dared to lay her own life on the line – treat herself (the author, not some other decorous character) as a representative figure. Authority may be a confidence trick, but we need it as a weapon against authority. As we approach the end of the twentieth century, and fundamentalisms, nationalisms and movements for Life revive, her demystificatory tactics seem less dated than they did.

Notes

1. Simone de Beauvoir, *The Force of Circumstance* (1963), trans. Richard Howard (New York: Putnam, 1976), p. 237.

2. Simone de Beauvoir, *When Things of the Spirit Come First* (1979), trans. Patrick O'Brian (London: Flamingo, 1982), p. 47.

3. Simone de Beauvoir, *The Prime of Life* (1960), trans. Peter Green (Harmondsworth: Penguin Books, 1962), p. 223.

4. Simone de Beauvoir, 'Mon experience d'écrivain' (1966), in Claude Francis and Fernande Gontier, *Les Écrits de Simone de Beauvoir* (Paris: Gallimard, 1979), pp. 439–57: 439: 'Écrire un roman, c'est en quelque sorte pulvériser le monde réel.'

5. Nathalie Sarraute, *Tropisms and The Age of Suspicion* (1939), trans. Maria Jolas (1950) (London: Calder and Boyars, 1959), pp. 32–3.

6. Roland Barthes, *Writing Degree Zero*, trans. Annette Lavers and Colin Smith (New York: Hill and Wang, 1968), p. 33.

7. Susan Rubin Suleiman, 'Simone de Beauvoir and the Writing Self', *L'Ésprit Créateur*, 29:4 (1989), 42–51: 46. I produced a fairly detailed analysis of Beauvoir's games with point of view in *She Came to Stay* in my book *Women in the House of Fiction* (London: Macmillan, 1992), where there is also a discussion of Beauvoir's refusal to celebrate a separate women's writing: see pp. 1–12.

8. He first made the point in the 1940s; see also, for example, Claude Lévi-Strauss, *Structural Anthropology* (1958), trans. C. Jacobson and B. Grundfest Schoepf (New York: Basic Books, 1963): 'it may be disturbing to some to have women conceived as mere parts of a meaningful system' (p. 61).

9. Toril Moi, *Simone de Beauvoir: The Making of an Intellectual Woman* (Oxford: Basil Blackwell, 1994), p. 66.

10. *Letters to Sartre* (1990), trans. Quintin Hoare (London: Radius, 1991), p. 451.

11 Elaine Marks, 'Transgressing the (In)cont(in)ent Boundaries: The Body in Decline', *Yale French Studies*, 72 (1986), 181–200: 193–4.

12 Angela Carter, *The Sadeian Woman* (London: Virago, 1979), p. 11.

13 'Must We Burn Sade?' (1953), in *Privilèges* (Paris: Gallimard, 1955), and in *Faut-il brûler Sade?*, Collection Idées (Paris: Gallimard, 1955).

14 Margaret Atwood, *Surfacing* (1973) (London: Virago, 1979), p. 181.

15 Margaret Atwood, *The Handmaid's Tale* (1985) (London: Virago, 1987), p. 83.

16 Nathalie Sarraute, *Portrait of a Man Unknown* (1948), trans. Maria Jolas (London: Calder and Boyars, 1963), p. 8.

17 Jean-Paul Sartre, *Being and Nothingness* (1943), trans. Hazel E. Barnes (London: Methuen, 1969), p. 609.

18 Moi, *Simone de Beauvoir*, p. 30.

19 Marks, 'The Body in Decline', pp. 189–90.

20 Judith Butler, 'Sex and Gender in Simone de Beauvoir's *Second Sex*', *Yale French Studies*, 72 (1986), 35–50: 45.

21 Ibid., p. 40.

22 Ibid., p. 48.

23 These arguments burgeoned in Judith Butler's *Gender Trouble: Feminism and the Subversion of Identity* (New York and London: Routledge, 1990) and *Bodies That Matter*, where she writes: 'Performativity describes this relation of being implicated in that which one opposes, this turning power against itself to produce alternative modalities of power': *Bodies That Matter* (New York and London: Routledge, 1993), p. 241.

24 *Adieux: A Farewell to Sartre* (1981), trans. Patrick O'Brian (London: André Deutsch and Weidenfeld and Nicolson, 1984), p. 125.

25 Christine Brooke-Rose, *Stories, Theories and Things* (Cambridge: Cambridge University Press, 1991), pp. 250–64.

26 Deirdre Bair, 'Simone de Beauvoir: Politics, Language and Sexual Identity', *Yale French Studies*, 72 (1986), 149–64: 154, n.

27 Phyllis Rose, *The Penguin Book of Women's Lives* (London: Viking, 1994), p. 19; the Kennedy Fraser quotation comes from *The New Yorker*, 6 November 1989.

28 Rose, *The Penguin Book of Women's Lives*, p. 24.

X

CHRISTINE BROOKE-ROSE

Remake

Christine Brooke-Rose's story of how this new book came to be is that she set out to write about her life, and instead produced a kind of antibiography. It's described in the jacket's blurb by Carcanel as 'an autobiographical novel with a difference' which 'uses life material to compose a third-person fiction'. Inside the covers we're told with confessional baldness that 'the old lady's publisher has asked for an autobiography. But the resistance is huge. The absorbing present creates interference, as well as the old lady's lifelong prejudice against biographical criticism, called laundry-lists by Pound. Only the text matters, if the text survives at all.' But then, isn't life always text for a Post-Structuralist? And then again, treating the facts as fiction doesn't seem exactly a major departure if *your fiction* is of the pared-down, see-through, new-novelish kind. Whichever way you look at it, Christine Brooke-Rose is on home ground in *Remake*: making it over is second nature to her.

She doesn't have a serious quarrel with most kinds of life-writing, of course, but that is a matter of genre. Which genre is such a text to claim kin with? What she objects to is treating life stories as romantic or realistic affairs. The writer she is, you gather, wouldn't be seen dead inhabiting such a plausible and formative life: that version of the Author is dead as a dodo for her. And that means questioning the importance of childhood, and the archetypal, claustrophobic family romance that's supposed to be so character-forming. Yes, it's significant that she grew up in various places – born in Geneva in 1926, brought up in Belgium and in England – but as much for the languages as for anything. There's no one mother-tongue in this story, to provide a starting-point, and no real father-figure either. Father was English, in fact, and early went missing, and you have to read between the lines pretty carefully to piece him together at all. 'A thief, a lying mythomaniac, a cheater', he's labelled in passing – a colourful, piratical parenthesis, no more. In fact, a younger and different Christine Brooke-Rose did once write up the adventure of the Search for Dad, in conventional style, in a novel called *The Dear Deceit*, in which she disguised herself as a male narrator and went to town on the details: dad had been a member of an Anglican Order, a kind of monk, and had run away and stolen the plate, and been sent to prison, among other picaresque episodes his wife and daughters only found out about after his desertion, and indeed after his death. *The Dear Deceit* was published in 1960, before she redefined herself as a writer (her first 'new' novel, *Out*, came out in 1964), and its use of real-life material is of the conventional kind – made over fully into fiction, with convincing characters and a questing plot. *That* father – in other words – was the father of a writer-daughter who was trying to fit herself into the conventional mould. Reborn, she refused to carry on the family 'line'. 'Forbidding but remarkable', said the *Telegraph* of *Out*, and *Punch* thought that the author was so sure of her new self that she must belong to the school of Samuel Beckett.

In *Remake* it's this wise child she celebrates, and indeed she mischievously cites – from Jenny Diski writing in the *London Review of Books*, as it happens – a witty mock-theory about the 'crucial years of an individual's psychological development not being from birth till five, but between the ages of 42 and 47'.

The psyche and personality in the first half of life would be merely malleable and unfinished, childhood trauma not trauma but neutral and neural experience. People would simply be analysed between the ages of 40 and 42 and get sorted out before the critical age – the Mid-Life Crisis – and be ready to spend fruitful years from middle age to death as positive, harmonious and psychologically healthy Houyhnhnms.

On this model, the move into reflexity that turned Brooke-Rose into an experimenter in fiction would figure as a kind of DIY analysis, at 40. However, as the tone suggests, this notion that we're born again at forty-something isn't meant entirely seriously (no one can be so taken with demystification as to find Houyhnhnms altogether congenial), and her childhood in the ordinary sense does after all get some space. In the beginning was language ('once upon a time there is a little girl born in French'), and early 'scatterings and smatterings' acquired in Geneva, Brussels and London, cherished mishearings and mistranslations: 'un fait divers is a winter fact'. The set-piece memory that stands in for a lot more, the only memory – we're told – 'still firm, personal and alive', is of grandmère's death in 1933. The old lady lies 'under an eiderdown of flowers, smelling of faint rot', and, terrifyingly, her eyes snap open to stare at her grand-daughter (disguised under the name of Tess) –

At supper grandpère asks Tess the colour of grandmère's eyes. Blue. Because grandpère's eyes are blue. Comment! Forgotten so soon? And Tess weeps into the bouillon, the tears joining the small golden rings of richness and the innumerable little letters made of pasta.

The scene has a sensuous force of conviction; you can see and hear and smell it. At the same time it's comically characteristic of Brooke-Rose that the alphabet pasta gets in, even here: the signature in memory's soup.

Most other early scenes flicker past, 'like forgotten photographs out of a drawer', and although she expresses some token regret for the vagaries of recall, the present-tense 'old lady' at her word-processor doesn't actually mind too much. Isn't life a story? she asks herself. And answers: No, life's a file – 'today all the terms for memory are spatial, screening, filing, effacing, storying, labelling, visualising, doors opening on doors'. The snapshots of the past are cross-cut with scenes from the present, the view from her windows, 'vineyards stretching towards the wooded hills of evergreen oak and pines . . . red and orange, the cherry-orchards dark crimson against the yellowing poplars', and this picturesque stuff is cross-cut in its turn with the polyglot TV babble and images of world news, for there's a vast dish on the roof now that she has 'all the time in the world to watch the world'. You're not allowed to forget for long that the work of memory is part of the same cartoon-strip, the same conspiracy to animate the still scenes and string them end to end. Do soap operas fit feminist theories about flux and fragmentation? Her own practice, in that case, is politically incorrect, for she feels compelled to register the ironies and absurdities and sleights of eye by which stories get sewn together, 'identities . . . a seamless tissue of half-lies'.

Still, this antibiography does follow a female 'line': mother's death is as memorable as grandmère's, indeed in some ways more so, for she dies 'bathed in love' in a Benedictine convent in London, at ninety-two. This after forty years as a nun, converted just after the war, when she is transformed from middle-aged, middle-class mummy to Mother Mary Anselm, leaving her two grown-up daughters strangely orphaned in the rejected 'world'. (Daddy dies – in a parenthesis, again, daddy *est mort* – back in 1934, but he's already 'been dead for ages' by then.) This time for mother's end there's a diary, 'a meditative account of a dying and a death, written between the acts', and this licenses a switch to the first person, for once. The only and vulnerable 'I' that suddenly appears in these pages isn't particularly eloquent, but does convey something of the anguish of losing a parent, even when you're middle-aged yourself, even when it's a death so long foreseen and so well prepared for. The loss is compounded, since this mother has so long been a stranger: 'They say she was always very strong, digging in the garden, working hard. As a young mother she was always exhausted . . . the nuns . . . file out, leaving me alone with her for a moment. I kiss her suddenly waxen brow. Outside, I cry out wildly against the wall, wondering at such pain.'

Perhaps the saddest aspect of this first-person confession of unbelief and grief is not her distance from her dying mother but her distance from her living sister, Joanne. Joanne (who has a restless, roving career) doesn't get much space altogether in the book, but she enters its pages like an avenging, intractable force. She writes hateful letters that this author, her sister, destroys – 'a totally mad, repulsive, compulsive, correspondence over forty years' – though a small specimen of her savagely sarcastic style survives to be quoted: 'How kind of you to have insisted – against everyone else's wishes – that I be summoned so's Mummy could see us both together, as I proposed to you, in writing, almost 2 years ago. Funny thing is that in a chat I had with the Ma P on arrival, she told me she'd done the insisting.'

Joanne is the bad sister, the guilty proof of one's failure as family, failure in closeness. She's also a reminder that

Brooke-Rose's experiments with breaking the rules don't just involve detached jokes about narrative strategy, but extend to the documentary transgression of kidnapping someone else's words on to the page. It's the middle-distance focus and the rounded character she wants to avoid, not the raw material of others and otherness. Joanne and 'I' are 'deeply different . . . from the first irreconcilable'. And you get the uncomfortable feeling that putting 'Joanne' in this book is part of an ongoing battle, no holds barred, no reconciliation achieved, mother's death just one in the series of sibling conflicts over space, 'this invented rivalry about happiness'.

After this episode even the book's customary third person seems to secrete a kind of insoluble solitariness. Brooke-Rose's habitual tone is a curious mixture – at once cosmopolitan and uncomfortably direct. She's in many ways cool and dry, and yet at the same time undefended, exposed. What's being deliberately stripped off (again) is the sociable, consistent carapace of a public personality – the sort of thing we rehearse for in the family, and which her family so signally fails to develop in her. Be that as it may, she contrives to take an overview of her life across the years without losing a sense of the oddness, partiality and contingency of its shape. One striking example of this is her account of the (de)forming of her sexual life because of an infantile love-affair with words. It starts with the seemingly harmless habit of sitting on her foot to hold in a full bladder, while listening to stories as a toddler, 'enjoying the fullness of the moment even with the fullness of the bladder'. This is in many ways so improbable that she had better tell it in her own words:

That heel-habit, formed for the prolongation of intellectual pleasures as the old lady knows full well, must have caused the so-called congenital malformation – *mais l'urèthre plonge dans le vagin* – blighting an entire sex life, not discovered by any English gyno or uro for over thirty years, found through the simplest fingerprod in Paris and fixed, decades too late. No wonder Tess rarely enjoyed sex . . . the child turned into an incongruous Sue Bridehead wanting only companionship, with sex as price to pay for love.

Neither using French nor taking the name of Thomas Hardy's heroine does much to dilute the painful intimacy of this. Why confide it? The graphic detail serves, seemingly, one major purpose for Brooke-Rose, which is to reveal herself as an author, as the self-made – or better, self-unmade – woman. Not therefore the creature of ready-made circumstances, or some mysterious fiat, some Godly dispensation, or some Freudian diagnosis. 'Congenital? Self-inflicted more likely?' If there is something nun-like and untouchable in her own character, like her mother's, then it has a particular, material ('neural and neutral') origin. She'll go a very long way, it seems, almost to any lengths, to avoid having a psyche or harbouring a soul.

The other main factor in shaping her sense of herself also has its strangeness, but it's a strangeness shared with quite a lot of other members of her wartime generation – a spell at Bletchley Park, decoding German signals: 'The young WAAF officer . . . reading and evaluating German messages all day for priority lists to the interpreters and cryptographers . . . The otherness of the other learnt young, the real war, seen from the enemy point of view.' It was, she says, her first university, and it made her aware of the power knowledge gives, especially knowledge out of the air, 'intercepted, decrypted, translated and transmuted'. Bletchley Park is an inspiration, more so, we gather, than the rather inept muse that's dictating poems to her at the time, on the side. Also on the side, she meets and marries and parts from her first husband, also at Bletchley, a wartime blip that leaves less of a trace than those airy messages – 'from the enemy viewpoint, the British being the enemy . . . the writer does that, learning to imagine the other. All human beings should . . . On the other hand, experiencing that same war as pure information . . . helps to turn Tess into a detached intellectual, never experiencing the grime, the cold, the heat.' On balance, and with Houyhnhnm hindsight, though, she's grateful for the training in seeing through the propaganda, especially when she contemplates the world her dish delivers to her retirement, 'the planet retribalised, everyone behaving as to the manna born'. The new media are cleverer not truer.

Her own cleverness gets her to Oxford after the war, where she takes up philology and enjoys watching the words cavort and shift and change: 'consonants breaking vowels, becoming mute, still there as dried-up foetuses in the spelling but unuttered'. She has met the love of her life by now, in more senses than one. There are the words; and there's the man, a Pole in exile, Janek, also an intellectual, also a writer, whom she meets and marries, and who transforms the world for her. This passage is written to match her euphoria; and also, since it's in the neo-romantic style of postwar poetry (David Gascoyne? Dylan Thomas? the Muriel Spark of those days, even?), to measure the distance between now and then: 'London is transformed. The red underground becomes blood thundering under London's skin . . . The stuttering sky full of birds plucks the eyes like parchment. A sigh sprinkles the night.' She isn't parodying her young self exactly, just observing the gap between. In 1957, quite a long time before the marriage fell apart, she would write *A Grammar of Metaphor*. The 'dissociation of mental and physical' is, alas, her lot – and despite her love for Janek, 'there's no dark Lawrentian passion for Tess'. Pretty soon, in the sixties, she'll write *Out* – and *Such and Between* – and (in 1968) be off on her own, to take up a university job at Paris VIII.

She found herself in the sixties, then, but in a characteristically oblique and ironic fashion, which had nothing much to do with liberation. And we stop there, really, since that's the point and focus of the book, the life of writing, the making of the writer. And yet, she contrives to the very end to sustain a teasing and troubling ambivalence on this very matter: are we getting only those aspects of the life that are relevant to the work? Or – as one comes increasingly to suspect – is this her real life, is this as real as it gets? The person she's writing about, and the one doing the writing, converge and mirror each other. And the portrait she gives of her present-tense self, sitting in her cottage in Provence with the dish on the roof channelling the world's images through her study, makes her out to be a kind of high-tech wise woman, like a figure from a twenty-first-century fairy tale – which is picturesquely pleasing, but doesn't resolve the matter of her good faith as a life-writer.

And perhaps it's unresolvable. After all, the question 'What is an author?' has become one of the most often asked and most unsatisfyingly answered questions of our times – whether you think of high theory, or the boom in literary biography, or the proliferation of readings and creative writing classes. What *Remake* does is to offer Christine Brooke-Rose's inconclusive evidence – her experience of making herself up. Her non-answer, though, has the edge on a lot of the answers to the author-question, precisely because of the way her theories and her practice coincide and collide and fertilise each other. It's a disconcerting performance – sometimes dry, sometimes moving, sometimes eccentric and evasive. But this is another way of saying that she leaves you wondering whether this is a book about someone experimenting in writing, simply *telling* it differently, or someone who experimented in living; and that uncertainty is exciting, like the unreasonable feeling of being on the verge (only on the verge, but never mind) of something new.

Textermination

The imaginative conceit on which Christine Brooke-Rose's new novel is based is at once witty and despairing. Characters from all the novels and stories you've ever read – and quite a few you haven't – gather in the San Francisco Hilton for the annual convention where they pray for Being, that they may live on for ever in the canon. Emma Woodhouse gets into the carriage with Mr Elton one more time, and find herself whisked off in a quite different direction, along with an elderly stranger speaking German, who is himself pursued by a large Lotte ('Wo ist Goethe?'), in a dress far too young for her, out of Thomas Mann. There is also *another* Emma whose skirts take up an inordinate amount of room, and who (what mortification!) languishes suggestively all over the place. Others climb into other vehicles: all the diligences, landaus, cabriolets and coaches that trundled the characters of the eighteenth and nineteenth centuries to their destinies and destinations converge now for the charter flight to Atlantic City, and thence to the West Coast. They are going to be interpreted; also to meet, flirt, argue and be taken on excursions to Death Valley and Silicon Valley, as conference-goers must.

They are the lucky ones, who come from realist texts. On the coast, they encounter hordes of two-dimensional beings who are in danger of fading away completely – figures out of classical epics, medieval romances, fables, legends and tales: and out of those twentieth-century novels where people are confused and fragmented and come ready-deconstructed like DIY kits. Or, simply buttonhole you and say 'I' all the time – though of course, that could be Tristram Shandy. Then there are the ones who spend all their time antisocially writing letters, some of them seem uncertain as to century. Whereas realist characters are impervious to time-travel. Emma herself, to great comic effect, remains as composed in the face of this novel's apocalyptic events (the earth *does* move) as she was during the Napoleonic wars. Nonetheless, the general picture darkens. The world of characters is overpopulated, and, at fiction's *fin-de-siècle* feast, the thin famished multitudes are pressing for attention and getting mutinous.

In *Textermination*, Christine Brooke-Rose is having punning fun with sacred convention. Let us play. Letting the characters out of the books isn't of course new – though the effect here is splendidly polymorphous-picturesque, a seminar in fancy-dress, fraught with possibilities of comic incomprehension and intrigues (Lancelot and Emma Bovary get on particularly well). What is new is that the joke this time isn't only against realism – rather, it's against the absurd solemnity with which the novel's latter-day experimenters and theoreticians have shouldered the white man's burden of deconstruction. For all the kowtowing to the Reader (in this book, people produce a vestigial genuflexion every time His name is invoked), the fiction that sets out to demystify authors, authority and illusion has been grossly and dogmatically self-obsessed. For Reader read the writer's ultimate wet dream of an infinitely patient, selfless, loving contortionist entirely given over to the pleasure of the text. At least the Muse was a flighty unpredictable type, and had to be wooed: the Reader, on the other hand, is generated by the words on the page and does what He (or is it perhaps She?) is asked:

all Eye (no 'I'). During Brooke-Rose's hilarious conference it is this Reader who is taken apart, dissolved, discredited. The characters start off the first session worshipping at a shrine which is 'like an open book, out of which stare innumerable eyes instead of letters', and intoning hopeful prayers to 'our Implied Reader, our Super Reader, our Ideal Reader, who gathers unto Himself all readers, and to His Interpreter, who gathers unto Himself all interpreters, of all interpretive communities'. But the service is interrupted by a band of Arab terrorists who object to the Judaeo-Graeco-Christian flavour of the proceedings, and are in search of a character called Gibreel Farishta, whom they plan to assassinate.

Readers with machine-guns, though, are only the extremist wing of the non-community of actual book-openers, who are splitting up along the fault-lines of creed, race and gender. Even in academe, they are inattentive and theory-blinded, or they yearn secretly for the old magical illusions; outside, they are refusing to play the game, watching television instead, reading (irony of ironies) writers' lives instead of their works. Brooke-Rose was one of the very few British writers who, in the 1960s, took up the challenge of the *nouveau roman* (in *Thru, Such*, and such); she also taught Anglo-American literature, and critical theory, at the University of Paris VIII, from 1968 until her recent retirement. She might therefore be expected to deplore this state of literary affairs rather than find it – as she clearly does – exhilarating. *Textermination*, though, is light-headed with a kind of terminal honesty. She has come through, after a life-time's love affair with the avant garde, with all her irreverence, her critical faculties and her creative ingenuity honed to a fine point. You couldn't call it a conversion, or even a loss of faith: what she has jettisoned is the dogmatism of unbelief.

Her most recent book of critical essays, *Stories, Theories and Things*, which was published in 1991, makes the point in a different way, by exploring how the canon works ('Outside the canon no interpretation ... outside the Church no salvation'), and the dubious dominance of academic criticism's 'self-perpetuating and confraternal industry', which ensures that certain books get attention, but treats them only generically, as allegories of fashionable *desiderata*. Thus compounding the postmodern condition in which 'we already know what each will say, each being no longer unique but returned to the emblematic, each a member of a class, a social, political or ideological group'. It should be evident that Brooke-Rose's concerns as critic and writer have converged into a volatile, anti-institutional cocktail. She knows what she's talking about, she's part of it: this fact gives her style a particular pungency. In an essay on character in fiction ('Which Way Did They Go? Thataways'), she remarks of contemporary novelists, 'We are in transition, no doubt, like the unemployed waiting for the newly structured technological society' and goes on to suggest mischievously that a combination of ill-matched influences from science fiction and feminism may provide the shape of things to come. Her point is that all the talk of otherness and difference must get down off its high horse: there is no universal Reader, only actual readers; the global village is a label. And 'there are many more interesting things to write about than the writer's difficulties with representation'.

This she has been working up to in her novels for some while. *Textermination* is the last of a loose quartet which started with *Amalgamemnon* (1984), went jokily science fiction with *Xorandor* (1986, kids meet computer-aliens, Enid Blyton meets Derrida), and continued in *Verbivore* (1990), with a glum fable about electronic media versus print and face-to-face talk. The continuing theme is the demise of humanism (there's a shadowy on-off narrator who is a redundant classics teacher) in the face of the plural and undecidable worlds of the present, all so available, yet so thin and hard to realize. The latest novel treats the topics of literary-critical debate as simply part of the scene 'outside'. The realist characters (Eurocentric first-worlders) are jostled by southern, eastern, alien figures; and all of them are elbowed aside by brash characters from television (Cultural Studies), who are fuelled by fears of mortality. Overpopulation, mutual incomprehension, rival schemes for grabbing attention ('The "I" narrators have formed an unofficial syndicate and are preparing for a coup'), inruption of the Unrepresented ('real' San Francisco gays), not to mention the terrorists, all create fast and furious narrative crises, fomenting and dissipating one after another in the Hilton lobby. The police arrive, but then they're all characters too, caught up in the same dance. Only at rare and improbable moments do the ill-assorted company catch a glimpse of peace – as when Prince Hordjedef, an ancient Egyptian-in-translation, pleads for calm – 'My father . . . believed that the future of the kingdom depended on stories . . . I also believe that the fate of the world depends, has always depended, on our ability to tell and to listen to stories. To listen, to believe, to suspend our customs of thought and let ourselves be charmed.' To that end, he introduces Princess Vidja, Ligaea, Scheherazade, who reduce the rioters to temporary calm, through 'enchantment and mesmerization'.

Unmistakably, however, the atmosphere is thickening into millennial chaos, and when the San Andreas fault opens up, like a latterday Pathetic Fallacy, in sympathy with the irretrievable dissension – the *deus ex machina* is a Tibetan monk who 'calls out a very long deep vowel to the universe' – the end is nigh. Picking their way over the rubble, the characters get back into their planes, balloons, coaches and carriages, and return to their books, some already coffins, others perhaps soon to become so. Emma is the last to leave, entering the carriage with Mr Elton following after as he always does. The last words – Jane Austen's – are: 'she would rather it had not happened'. Actually, Emma has had a good time, without stepping in the least out of character. And so had Christine Brooke-Rose, though she *has* stepped out of character on to the reader's territory (as opposed to the Reader's), to reveal herself as a most ingenious entertainer, a demystifier of the demystifiers (who expect you to accept *their* stories about stories), plentiful of plot and generously diverting.

Christine Brooke-Rose and Contemporary Fiction

'Outside the canon no interpretation . . . outside the Church no salvation.' This was Christine Brooke-Rose, speaking about the fate of her own fiction in her critical book, *Stories, Theories and Things*, in 1991. Her double career as critic and novelist was the source of not a little ironical reflection: more people read her criticism. When she came to mull over her relations with the readers and critics of her other, creative self over the years, she was bound to conclude, with characteristic frankness, that her 'reception' hadn't been exactly a success story. Would Brooke-Rose the novelist be one of the saved? Highly unlikely. But she was prematurely pessimistic, for here comes a critical study of her oeuvre, in which the very neglect of her creative work supplies a theme.

Looking back, as Sarah Birch does in *Christine Brooke-Rose and Contemporary Fiction*, with hindsight, you can spot, even in the Christine Brooke-Rose of the 1950s, the embryonic maverick who would become defiantly and terminally 'experimental'. On the face of things she was doing everything in the conventionally right way – writing like a realist; expressing (actually repressing) any doubts by being humorous, witty and 'light'; and writing reviews on the side, making a place for herself in the London literary world. But as Birch is able to show without too much difficulty, the general malaise that afflicted realistic fiction in the period, so that it became either exaggeratedly 'manly' ('angry'), or playfully allegorical and metaphysical (Angus Wilson, Iris Murdoch), invaded Brooke-Rose's early work like a debilitating virus. She couldn't – like Wilson and Murdoch – make literary capital out of the decay of plausibility. Or wouldn't. Nor did she, like her friend Muriel Spark, go the whole hog and write metafiction about relations between authors and God (though we're told she flirted with Catholicism). Instead, she produced irritable, elliptical books, that fell between two stools. The best of them, *The Languages of Love* (1957) and *The Dear Deceit* (1960), are indeed – you can now see – understated anti-novels in which, as Birch says, 'the pretence of representing lived reality begins its slow death'. Neither, though, is as good as her trail-blazing critical book of 1958, *The Grammar of Metaphor*. It was the secret life of words that excited her.

That was not, given her background, entirely surprising. For a start she grew up speaking English, French and German (her mother was Swiss, her father English), and lived in Belgium and Switzerland during her childhood. Her war-work was decoding German communications, her subsequent academic education at Oxford and then London centred on philology, and while she was a student she married the exiled Polish writer Jerzy Pietrkiewicz. She was thus herself a kind of displaced person even before a severe illness in 1962, together with an immersion in the *nouveau roman*, set her thinking more impersonally about the character of authorship. There followed *Out* (1964), *Such* (1966) and *Between* in 1968, in which year she parted company with her husband, and England, and took up the teaching post at the Sorbonne (American Literature, Literary Theory) which she held for twenty years until her retirement. She continued to write in English, though, or mostly – *Between*, which features a love-affair between translators, is in several languages, and takes place airily in transit, on planes, in hotels – and there's the rub. For while you can show that in theory Brooke-Rose has been exploring exactly the right themes for our postmodern, deconstructive era, in fact English readers (English-language readers) haven't made much mental room for her.

The problem of course is that if you're to write literary history you need to be something of a realist. Brooke-Rose's career in fact involves a kind of double-take about realism. Why was she so charmed by the notion of the novel as the site of verbal play, by polyglossia, by split 'selves' and by puns? Because, I would think – compare Nathalie Sarraute – it promised a kind of liberation from origins, from 'place', in the form of gender, class, nation. Brooke-Rose longed, in her fiction of the 1960s and 70s, for what Roland Barthes called textual *atopia*, placelessness. And in the best of the novels since then – particularly *Amalgamemnon* (1984), *Xorandor* (1986) and *Textermination* (1991) – she has been ruefully, and sometimes hilariously, reassessing her position. Even placelessness must have, it turns out, a place on the *literary* map. Her splendid essay 'Illiterations', all about the problems of being an experimental *woman* writer, reinstates the gender issue with a vengeance: and a more impersonal piece on 'Palimpsest History' as the distinctive genre of much of the most interesting contemporary fiction does the same for national 'stories'. Thinking again (and she's a devastatingly clear thinker, even if the result is to marginalise her own work), she sees that the idea that fiction was becoming a kind of laboratory where you could impartially expose the present-tense relational structures of language was mistaken. In the event, for instance, the avant-garde writers who spoke with authority *against* authority turned out to be men. All those metaphors about the 'canon' should be taken seriously: originality is still in many contexts assumed to he mysteriously *male*. (Compare the fuss about ordaining women as priests.)

Brooke-Rose goes further here towards explaining the difficulty of 'placing' her kind of work. And if you add in some more biographical and circumstantial detail – behave more like a realist – you can make her sound in her own weird way plausible, and so place her displacement. It has to be interesting, surely, that the rogue father whose life formed the biographical basis for the plot of *The Dear Deceit* started off as a monk (but stole the monastery silver); and that her mother, after his death, became a nun? (No wonder she's out to demystify origins.) Also, that the war-work took place at the famous decoding centre at Bletchley. Also, that she was a friend of both Muriel Spark and Anthony Burgess, and indeed wrote a very funny short story about Spark and success ('Queenie Fat and Thin') which is less than purely atopian. Birch is right to imply that Brooke-Rose ought to fit the fashionable desiderata – Bakhtin, Kristeva, etc. But the paradox is that you can only exist as a writer if you have a 'voice' for your readers, and Brooke-Rose's voice has seemed more distant and characterless than in fact it is, particularly since – and this is far from being an incidental fact about 'the literary industry' – she has not been around in this country to do interviews and readings from her work. It's arguable that so-called experimental fiction, being in some sense more like poetry, actually needs to be read aloud to live in readers' heads – a special and pleasing irony, when you consider that it's a throwback to orality, this tradition, and diametrically opposed to deconstructionist notions that it's the written word that liberates multiple plays of meaning.

One strong argument for adding Brooke-Rose into the contemporary canon is that she raises such interesting questions on the boundaries of the theory and practice of fiction-writing. I cannot help feeling that she remains her own best critic, a splendidly reluctant convert to the necessity of being someone at last.

Next

Christine Brooke-Rose's new novel is set in London, and wanders the streets with the unemployed and the homeless, who pass on the burden of telling the story to one another like a baton in some shambling relay race. It's a very realist topic for a notoriously anti-realist writer – Beckett meets *Bleak House* – but on reflection there's an impeccable logic in Brooke-Rose's identification with her derelicts. These rough sleepers and monologists, like the New Novelists of the 1950s and 1960s, have lost the plot and the conviction of having characters. And they are no longer *the* representative outsiders, but part of a contemporary social map that's so big and bitty that it has no real outside.

Experimental writing, to spell out a rueful analogy, is no longer the Other, any more than the poor. Isn't everyone a bit tricky these days, a bit insecure, a bit playful, a bit between? 'No lumpen proles only lumpen bourgeoisie.' All of which means that a writer like Christine Brooke-Rose is marginalised in a new way – there is something literal and intransigent and unfashionable about her insistence that the poor are indeed *without*. This book denies itself the use of the verb 'to have' to make the point, and mimics graphically on the page the solitary wanderings of its people, with sentences that string themselves out like old concrete poems (as unloved and out of date as tower-blocks), and have no 'I' in them, since an 'I' depends on a 'you' to talk to, and only materialises when they run into each other in hostels and job centres and doorways: 'You're there and I talk.'

But their contacts are fleeting. One of the novel's funnier and sadder observations is that isolation is so addictive it's often irreversible, it makes you at once hungry for company and unable to cope with it. Given half a chance, some of these people — the ex-teacher who spent most of his life in Africa, for instance — will bore any interlocutor silly. 'He talks he talks, he talks like a book, them questions was just to get the ole self on,' says a young black truant and apprentice rapper who's implausibly patient with the opinionated old buffer, in order to enable him to spell out another of the book's themes: 'the way we talk is only the dialect we were born and brought up in ... Did you ever read Scott ...?' The nearest thing to a shared language they have is what the didactic buffer calls Estuarian, the post-Cockney demotic of the South-East. Brooke-Rose transcribes it on the page in mockery of the old certainties of place and class — 'Jes lahk laif inni?' And the alienation-effect *is* real, a continuous grating on the reader's imaginary ear, the noise of Streetland, where people might as well all be plugged into Walkmans.

When Dickens asked himself and his readers in *Bleak House* what connection there could possibly be between illiterate, orphaned, lost Jo the crossing-sweeper and (say) Lady Dedlock, it was an archly rhetorical question. Jo proves his kinship by contagion, do-gooding Esther Summerson catches his smallpox, is revealed as Lady Dedlock's illegitimate daughter, which in turn provides a motive for the murder of lawyer Tulkinghorn, which eventually enables Inspector Bucket and the author to tie everything up. Here, the needy and marginal compete with and prey on each other, the murder that's the main event is unsolved, there's a diaspora of destinies. At the end, we levitate into a curious, elegaic poetry, a hypothermic dream:

<blockquote>

days
                              hours
(Is there a life before death?)
                    under the lullaby of trucks
          as the snow, thickening fast, the now slanting snow,
                    greypinkly eiderdowns him over . . .
     to be debriefed by eternity
                                   but with no next.
</blockquote>

We'll take a break now. Stay with them.

Next is a moving book, despite its dryness and deliberation. Christine Brooke-Rose is a foreigner herself in London. She has lived and worked in France for thirty years now, and she looks at the city with an unaccommodated eye, charting its long decay as the capital of an empire of signs – which is (paradoxically enough) something that she takes absolutely personally.

XI

IRIS MURDOCH

Obituary

Iris Murdoch kept a faith in the novel's continuity and vitality alive, not only by inventing her own rich recipe – densely-populated, hybrid, dangerous and celebratory – but by simply doing it again and again. Her fertility of invention, her addictive and throwaway plots, the endless difference one from another of her characters, spelled out a cryptic consistency people counted on. So although she sometimes claimed to be a realist, it was the reality of her energy and conviction that gave the claim meaning, as much as the form the books took. She was in many ways unworldly, but not when it came to work. She praised concreteness and concentrated on the practical processes of illusion-making, always to be done again if you want to keep the show on the road, from the beginning of her career right through to the end.

In *Under the Net* (1954), her first published novel, her narrator Jake starts out in love with avant-garde abstraction. He ends up opening a book by a best-selling author whose work he has been translating and despising, and gets a whiff of authentic enchantment: 'The style had hardened, the manner was confident, the pace long and slow . . . Starting a novel is like opening a door on a misty landscape, you can still see very little, but you can smell the earth and feel the wind blowing.' Jake was discovering his own and his author's vocation. More than thirty years later, in *The Book and the Brotherhood* her character Gerard recalled that marvellous beginning – 'It's gone, he thought, the past, it is irrevocable and beyond mending and far away, and yet it is here, blowing at one like a wind, I can feel it, I can smell it, and it's so sad . . .' When Alzheimer's meant she was no longer able to write, her husband John Bayley's memoir *Iris* kept her alive as one of the characters of love she'd created as fictions, and he'd written about as a critic. And now the obituaries talk about the loss of a particular link with tradition. All we have is the words on the page to play with, and where does posterity start?

One obvious answer is where she did: not with novel-writing, but with her 1953 book on Sartre (she'd been a Philosophy Fellow at Oxford since 1948), and the beginning of her battle with utopian anti-art, very much a battle *with* in the sense that she was endlessly tempted by asceticism, puritanism, iconoclasm, conviction so pure you could dispense with things and with other people. 'Dostoevsky says', says someone in her 1970 novel *A Fairly Honourable Defeat*, 'that plain truth is so implausible that most people instinctively mix in a little falsehood.' But though you might think, taking this out of context, that we're bound to deplore this grubby habit, it's not so obvious that it's a bad thing. Plain truth is a kind of perilous mirage, you can't possess it. And lies are the foundation of the novelist's art: in the Sartre book she argues that it's the lack of concrete illusion and sympathy with human muddle in the work of Sartre the novelist that reveals the limitations of the existential project as Sartre the philosopher understands it. He has 'an impatience, which is fatal to the novelist proper, with the *stuff* of human life', he doesn't convey – doesn't really see – 'the absurd, irreducible otherness of people, and of their relations to each other'. She is very funny about the startling passages in *Being and Nothingness* on slime, the horrible (feminine, clinging, compromising) stickiness of the world outside oneself: 'These evocations of the viscous, the fluid, the paste-like sometimes achieve a kind of horrid poetry . . .' Her own earlier novels are all kind to matter, to the 'stuff' of life. In *The Red and the Green* in 1965, her only historical novel, set in Ireland (both her father and mother were Irish Protestants, though she grew up English), she produced a marvellous set-piece in praise of the Muse of muddle:

> Blessington Street . . . had, under the pale bright sky, its own quiet air of dereliction, a street leading nowhere, always full of idle dogs and open doorways . . . Looked at closely, the bricks of these houses showed in fact a variety of colours, some purplish red, some yellowish grey, all glued together by a jelly of filth to form a uniform organic surface rather like the scales of a fish, the basic material of Dublin, a city conjured from the earth all in one piece by some tousled Dido.

The book's plot exposes the fanaticism of the man in love with a cause, the abstract man, heroic terrorist Pat Dumay, who wishes he was bodiless, and hates women for being 'muddled and unclean, representative of the frailty and incompleteness of human life'. *The Red and the Green* wasn't in fact one of her best, since its celebration of human jumble was overschematic. But it helps underline the point that she began with the assumption – a product of the 1930s political climate and the war, and prophetic of things to come – that radical cleansing is at some level what we're programmed to want. The trick her novels aim to pull off is not to make order, but to complicate order in such a way that it starts to resemble living.

She often used her own special, fishy body-language: 'Each human being swims in a sea of faint suggestive imagery. It is this web of pressures, currents and suggestions . . . which ties our fugitive present to our past and future . . .' Here again there's the characteristic paradox that she's generalising about the importance of being particular. She is marvellously sensuous about skin, hair, eyes, clothes, pictures, possessions, food without pointing the moral, though. Her characters covet beautiful things and beautiful people, and erotic art-works where the two are superimposed – 'The marble was warm and golden and very slightly rough. The modelling of the figure had an exquisiteness of sensitive detail which gave itself voluptuously to the questing finger tips . . .' Still and all it's probably the inverse attraction of the revolting that she does most memorably – the awful meals Charles Arrowby gloatingly prepares for himself in *The Sea, the Sea* (which won the Booker in 1978), or the kitchen (*A Fairly Honourable Defeat* again) where Tallis, a good man though no saint, does his thinking:

The sink was piled with leaning towers of dirty dishes . . . The dresser was covered in a layer, about a foot high, of miscellaneous oddments, books, papers, string, letters, knives, scissors, elastic bands, blunt pencils, broken biros, empty ink bottles, empty cigarette packets and lumps of old hard stale cheese. The floor was not only filthy, but greasy and sticky and made a sucking sound as Hilda lifted her feet . . .

Murdoch novels are decorated and furnished with a kind of perverse elegance: a Greek *kouros* and unwashed milk-bottles, plastic flowers and Shakespearean quotations.

She's a genius with lists, like Dickens and Joyce – and obviously her early, slim books owed a good deal to Beckett, and Raymond Queneau – but it's surprisingly hard to identify the fictional forebears she brought herself up on. Scott, Tolstoy, George Eliot, Dostoevsky, Melville, Hawthorne, Stevenson? Her characters often seem to belong to Bloomsbury, but she doesn't write like Forster or Woolf. Shakespeare and Romantic poets seem closer to the mark; and closer still late classical 'novels' like Petronius' *Satiricon* and Apuleius' *The Golden Ass*, with their erotic metamorphoses and ambivalent oracles. And, of course, Plato's dialogues. Certainly the thinker she found most provocative and congenial was Plato, and she set up a kind of dialogue with him because he seemed an exemplary utopian who – in banishing the artists – did acknowledge how very dangerous to the pursuit of purity artistic representations could be. In her book on him, *The Fire and the Sun* (1977), she converts Plato's claustrophobic cave of the benighted, who are hypnotised by the world's spectacle, into 'a great hall of reflection where we can all meet and and where everything under the sun can be examined and considered'. Reflection here is a kind of pun on thought and mirrors: mirrors flatter our delusions but most of us probably can't think without them. We know ourselves best in images that are ambiguous, hypothetical, provisional. She writes reverently of 'the pierced nature of the work of art, its limitless connection with ordinary life'. This is what leaches away visionary certainties. But at the same time she's taking for granted that often the best people are half in love with abstractions. Conversely, the love-affair with theory was rooted in erotic attraction for Socrates and for Plato: no brain-children without beautiful boys to help you conceive them.

She contemplated art history as a profession, and Renaissance allegorical paintings and tapestries often act as mirrors for the people inside her books, as do Shakespeare's plays. In fact, she's rather like a Renaissance Neo-Platonist, the kind who justified physical desire and the lust of the eyes by saying that the images were rungs on a ladder; doubtless when you became a Socratic saint, you'd kick the ladder and the habit of wanting away, but meanwhile . . . '"Falling in love" . . . is for many people the most extraordinary and vivid experience of their lives, whereby the centre of significance is suddenly ripped out of the self . . .' Her character Bradley Pearson in *The Black Prince* (1973), who is a madman and a liar with more than a touch of Nabokov's Humbert Humbert about him, fills out this idea: 'Why cannot this release from self provide a foothold in a new place which we can then colonize and enlarge until at last we will *all* that is not ourselves. That was Plato's dream.' In the age-old rivalry between the artists and the philosophers, she came down on the side of traditional artists as in a way *better philosophers*, better at 'picturing consciousness', and in this she found herself at odds with the reverence for theory in the intellectual climate of our times. Radical deconstructionists she associated with ancient paradox-mongers who savoured infinite regress, infinite deferral, like Zeno. Reflexivity, self-consciousness, stasis she feared and evaded. In *The Book and the Brotherhood* someone says 'Plato did a good job when he threw out the preSocratics.' 'Yes,' is the rejoinder, 'but they're back.'

Her novels are dialogues with her readers, their plots and portraits are for provocation, seduction, consumption rather than contemplation. In *The Flight from the Enchanter* (1956), which people now think is probably her earliest fiction – or the earliest to survive – though it wasn't published first, the juvenile lead recalls a visit to her brother, who has found his spiritual home in Paris:

Annette had had to spend many evenings . . . listening to endless conversations which went on into the morning hours until the air was so thick with abstractions that she fell, half stifled, into a comfortless sleep . . . '*Moi, j'aime le concret!*' she had cried out, waking suddenly at the end of one of these sessions. '*Le concret! C'est ce qu'il y a de plus abstrait!*' her brother had replied smartly. Everyone laughed and Annette burst into tears.

Her brother is right, at least as far as Murdoch's concrete details are concerned, they are shot through with abstract meaning, they are allegorical. But Annette is right, too, to talk about love, which is what ties them into body-language. It's pleasing to imagine her as an avatar of her author (who had no siblings) – 'Like Nike, she was normally to be seen in rapid motion, putting her foot to the ground in a whirl of drapery. Annette wore underneath her dress two or three coloured petticoats; so that as she ran . . . her long legs appeared in a kaleidoscope of whirling colours.' Annette here is an untidy combination of the Winged Victory and Iris the Rainbow Goddess – a good emblem of someone who liked to keep one jump ahead of solemnity. This particular book, which makes use of some violent material that seems to have been gleaned from Murdoch's work for the United Nations agency dealing with displaced persons and refugees at the end of the war, has a more grown-up heroine called Rosa (after Rosa Luxemburg), who works on a factory production-line to appease her conscience, but has there a saving erotic encounter Murdoch describes with panache – 'Jan still had his left had on the lever; Rosa's hand covered his, and for a moment she felt the steel of the lever through his flesh . . .'

It won't do to end on this bawdy note. Iris Murdoch's work will survive precisely because it spans an extraordinary range, which includes high seriousness. You can see her influence not only in the work of someone like A. S. Byatt, who has always acknowledged her as a mentor, or the first novels of both

A. N. Wilson (*The Sweets of Pimlico*) and Candia McWilliam (*A Case of Knives*), which were tributes, but also in the fiction of writers as diverse as Alan Hollinghurst and Marina Warner. She bridged theory and practice in a unique way. Her description of one of her characters in the early *Enchanter* book fits her too: 'Here was a personality without frontiers.'

XII

ANGELA CARTER

The Fairy Tale

You mention folk culture and people immediately assume
you're going to talk about porridge and clog-dancing . . .
                                        Angela Carter, 1991

Nineteen seventy-nine was Angela Carter's *annus mirabilis* as a
writer, the hinge-moment or turning point when she invented
for herself a new authorial persona, and began for the first time
to be read widely and *collusively*, by readers who identified with
her as a reader and re-writer. New wine in old bottles was
already one of her most serviceable slogans for her practice as
a novelist, but now she gave roots and a rationale to her habitual
vein of fantasy, parody and pastiche. In the two slim books
she published that year, *The Bloody Chamber* and *The Sadeian
Woman*, she explained herself, unpacked her gifts, played her
own fairy godmother. She had already published seven novels
and a book of stories. In fact, she would produce only two
more novels, one more collection of short fiction and another
of journalism before she died in 1992. But the really magical
thing about the books of 1979 was this: they not only heralded
her carnival transformation in *Nights at the Circus* (1984) and
Wise Children (1991), but they gave back her earlier work to
herself and her readers, the re-writer re-read and canonised. She
had started out as a member of the 1960s counterculture – 'the

savage sideshow' as she wryly called it – but twenty years on she no longer looked marginal at all.[1] The present essay sets out to explore some of the implications of this story, and the role fairy tales played in it.

Marina Warner, herself much affected and influenced by the post-1979 Carter – Warner described *From the Beast to the Blonde: On Fairy Tales and Their Tellers* (1994) as inspired by the writing of Angela Carter (in Sage, *Flesh and the Mirror*) – saw Carter's relation to this genre as an affair of the heart: 'Fairy tales explore the mysteries of love . . . Angela Carter's quest for Eros, her attempt to ensnare its nature in her imagery . . . drew her to fairy tales as a form . . .' But it was just as much an affair of the head, motivated by what Carter called in a 1989 review of Pavic's *Dictionary of the Khaẓars* 'the cerebral pleasure of the recognition of patterning afforded by formalism' (Carter, *Expletives Deleted*). In her work, she valued and sought abstraction as an antidote to the climate of foggy realism in which she'd grown up. And in this she resembled, as she herself saw, such writers as Italo Calvino, whose story also highlighted the transformative effects of his rediscovery of fairy tales and folktales (Carter, 'Angela Carter Interviewed by Lorna Sage').[2]

'When I began my career, the categorical imperative of every young writer was to represent his own time . . .' Calvino wrote, looking instead to time past and to the future, in *Six Memos for the Next Millennium*. The 1956 collection of Italian folktales he edited (and re-wrote out of their various dialects into Italian) had seeped into the structure and texture of his own work, and given him the clue to a different dialogic relation to readers (most obviously in the fragmentary, permutable *Invisible Cities* in 1972 and in *If on A Winter's Night a Traveller* in 1979). 'If . . . I was attracted by folktales and fairy tales, this was not the result of loyalty to an ethnic tradition . . . nor the result of nostalgia for things I read as a child,' he explained in his lecture on the narrative virtue of 'Quickness': 'It was rather because of my interest in style and structure.' He was in rebellion against the postwar socialist-realist orthodoxy, which preached that the artist could only connect himself with 'the people' if he wrote naturalistically. The folktale suggested a different way of thinking about this: the craft of storytelling as practised by people themselves had been once upon a time on the side of fantasy and recursive patterns. Choosing to evade 'the weight, the inertia, the opacity of the world' (Calvino) wasn't escapist or decadent, and quite the opposite of an addiction to Art for Art's sake:

> I am accustomed to consider literature as a search for knowledge . . . as extended to anthropology and ethnology and mythology. Faced with the precarious existence of tribal life – drought, sickness, evil influence – the shaman responded by ridding his body of weight and flying to another world. In centuries and civilizations closer to us, in villages where the women bore most of the weight of a constricted life, witches flew by night on broomsticks, or even on lighter vehicles such as ears of wheat or pieces of straw. Before being codified by the Inquisition, these images were part of the folk imagination . . . (Calvino)

This tale about the origin of 'Lightness', a tale about the pretexts of tales, resembles Carter's own position on the matter; in the Preface to the first of the two collections of fairy tales she edited for Virago, she wrote that fairy tales and folktales represent 'the most vital connection we have with the imaginations of the ordinary men and women whose labour created our world . . .' In *The Sadeian Woman*, more peremptorily, she said: 'If nobody, including the artist, acknowledges art as a means of *knowing* the world, then art is relegated to a kind of rumpus room of the mind.' Like pornography, the fairy tale was practical fantasy, in this view, and it worked by narrative levitation – abstraction, patterning, getting above yourself . . .

Well, up to a point, and depending on who you were. Calvino, who had spent the boom years of structuralist theory in Paris, refers us to Propp's *Morphology of the Folktale* (1968): '[I]n folktales a flight to another world is a common occurrence. Among the "functions" catalogued by Vladimir Propp . . . it is one of the methods of "transference of the hero", defined as follows: "Usually the object sought is in 'another' or 'different' realm that may be situated far away horizontally, or else at a great vertical depth or height".' You can see how this schema would have appealed to Calvino, since he has already described his cast of mind in the 1940s – 'the adventurous, picaresque rhythm that prompted me to write' – at the time he set out on his own anti-realist quest for identity as a writer. But for the female reader/writer, surely the case is altered? Most of Propp's examples, as Jack Zipes points out in *Don't Bet on the Prince* (1986), contain a very different pattern of signification for girls and women: 'What is praiseworthy in males . . . is rejected in females; the counterpart of the energetic, aspiring boy is the scheming, ambitious woman . . . Women who are powerful and good are never human . . .' Zipes, a scholar of the fairy tale, is also a self-confessed fan of Carter's work; and indeed the cheerful confidence of his tone here owes a lot to her arguments and example. Carter, of course, hadn't put her money on the prince. The hero of transference almost never I think appears in her own fairy tales, except possibly in the guise of Puss-in-Boots, an agile, resourceful tom who scales rococo and neoclassical façades with great panache; and just possibly as the cyclist hero of 'The Lady of the House of Love', whose bicycle replaces seven-league boots. In the novels, he's represented by Desiderio in *The Infernal Desire Machines of Dr Hoffman* (1972) and by Walser (in *Nights at the Circus*, 1984) – especially the latter, who is apprenticed to a shaman on his fumbling way to becoming a fit mate for the winged heroine Fevvers, who is indeed powerful and good and not exactly human.[3]

During the 1970s, Carter had been re-reading fairy tales and Sade in tandem, and bleakly contemplating the fate of good, powerless girls, the Red Riding Hoods and Sleeping Beauties of the world. She practised a deliberate and reductionist habit of interpretation. In *The Sadeian Woman*, there are many occasions when she refers to 'bankrupt enchantments' and 'fraudulent magic':

> To be the *object* of desire is to be defined in the passive case.
>
> To exist in the passive case is to die in the passive case – that is, to be killed.
>
> This is the moral of the fairy tale about the perfect woman.

You could argue that she's here merely using the term 'fairy tale' in its colloquial sense: a sugar-coated lie; or more grandly, a 'myth', a cultural construct naturalised as a timeless truth. But the profile of the passive heroine is too close to too many fairy-tale characters to sustain the distinction. Sade, Carter argues, has this to be said for him: that in the person of his long-suffering heroine Justine he 'contrived to isolate the dilemma of an emergent type of woman. Justine, daughter of a banker, becomes the prototype of two centuries of women who find the world was not, as they had been promised, made for them . . . These self-consciously blameless ones suffer and suffer until it becomes second nature . . .' (*The Sadeian Woman*).[4] You can find this woman in conduct books, novels, psychoanalysis and suburbia as well as in pornography. And the fairy tale too has come to serve this post-romantic-agony culture that is modern and masochistic at once. Carter had always played with other 'genres' – the Gothic, science fiction – which belong to this Sadeian moment. Women writers (for example, Ann Radcliffe and Mary Shelley) are hugely inventive in these genres, but they don't afford the formal distance of the fairy tale, which has a longer and larger history.

So fairy tale has here a two-faced character. Its promiscuity – the stories are anybody's – means that you do have to understand it historically, as drawn into the sensibility of the times, more often than not as a supporting strand in a realist or sentimental bourgeois narrative. But you can tease out the sub-text; and in any case older, sparer tales, and alternative tellings, surviving ghettoised in the nursery or in folklore collections alongside their assimilated versions, contrive (like Sade's repetitive and obscene narratives) to isolate their elements for cruelly lucid contemplation. The one thing you mustn't do is mistake the endless recurrence of these characters and these plots for evidence of the universal cultural passivity of women in the past.[5] In fairy tales once upon a time people *could* see the wood for the trees. And so Carter, while registering with grim humour and clarity the awful legacy of 'the fairytale about the perfect woman', still sees in the genre a means by which a writing woman may take flight. Gender-politics don't undo the formal appeal of the fairy tale, though they do mean you have to take a longer detour through cultural history to arrive at lightness.

In 1978, in her radio play *Come unto These Yellow Sands*,

Carter has one of the products of Victorian fairyland, Oberon (as characterised by Shakespeare-as-seen-by-painter-Richard Dadd), give an indignant revisionist lecture (to an audience of goblins, elves and other disenfranchised figments) about the history of 'fairy subjects'. Oberon's line is a post-Marxist one: the ascendant middle classes lived off the imaginative labour of the poor, just as they lived off their physical labour:

> The primitive superstitions of the countryside, the ancient lore born on the wrong side of the blanket to religious faith, could not survive in the smoke, the stench, the human degradation ... of the great cities ... Here the poor were stripped of everything, even of their irrational dreads, and the external symbols of their dreams and fears ... were utilized to provide their masters with a decorative margin of the 'quaint', the 'fanciful' and the 'charming' ... This realm of faery served as a kitsch repository for fancies too savage, too dark, too voluptuous, fancies that were forbidden the light of common Victorian day *as such.* (*Yellow Sands*)

The phrase 'kitsch repository' anticipates *The Sadeian Woman*'s 'rumpus room of the mind'. But that is indeed where you have to rummage if you want to retrieve art as 'a way of *knowing* the world'. This didactic radio-play Oberon is a very apposite (and funny) exponent of the revisionist analysis of fairy tale as a means of knowledge and of *self-knowledge*. When he describes Victorian fairyland as 'a kind of pornography of the imagination' he is pointing to its last link with reality, its saving gracelessness.

In this sense, 'genre' retains its own separate power: like pornography, fairy tale relies on repeated motifs, multiple versions and inversions, the hole in the text where the readers insert themselves. Its availability to interpretation, its *potential* poverty, bareness, lightness, represent the possibility of rendering the obsessive matter of cruelty, desire and suffering (which is mainstream fiction's fantastical and Gothic underside) profane and provisional. In his 1979 book *Breaking the Magic Spell*, Jack Zipes wrote that 'the best of folk and fairy tales chart ways for us to become masters of history . . . they transform time into relative elements'. They are an antidote to eternity, in other words, 'born on the wrong side of the blanket from religious faith'. And in this as in other ways, re-reading them is an *Enlightenment* project. In a 1978 interview, Carter said, about Sade, 'He's sent me back to the Enlightenment, where I am very happy. They mutter the age of reason is over, but I don't see how it ever began so one might as well start again, now. I also revere and emulate Sade's rigorous atheism . . .' Carter habitually associated the prestige and glamour of passivity with the cult of Christianity and Father Gods in general, and was also deeply unsympathetic to the idea of their replacement with Mothers: 'If women allow themselves to be consoled for their culturally determined lack of access to the modes of intellectual production by the invocation of hypothetical great goddesses, they are simply flattering themselves into submission . . . Mother goddesses are just as silly a notion as father gods' (*The Sadeian Woman*).

One of the reasons she so valued fairy tale – and one that is obscured by a too-exclusive focus on gender-politics – is that she associated it with a world where our dreads and desires were personified in beings that were not-human without being divine. Kurt Vonnegut used to make the same point in his oft-delivered vaudeville routine about writing an anthropology dissertation for his MA (rejected), drawing graphs of the story-lines of our Western myths and favourite legends. He discovers that the Bible story produces the same pattern as 'Cinderella', with the risen Christ as Prince Charming:

> The steps . . . are all the presents the fairy godmother gave to Cinderella, the ball gown, the slippers, the carriage, and so on. The sudden drop is the stroke of midnight. All the presents have been repossessed. But then the prince finds her and marries her, and she is infinitely happy ever after. She gets all the stuff back and *then* some. A lot of people think this story is trash, and, on graph paper, it certainly looks like trash . . . But . . . then I saw that the rise to bliss at the end was identical with the expectation of redemption . . . The tales were identical. (Vonnegut)[6]

Sade and *The Bloody Chamber* combined provided Carter with a potted history of 'fantasy'; and also with a new vantage point on her own marginality, a new way of understanding it as not the position of a *literary* victim or decadent. Nineteen seventy-nine was the year of Gilbert and Gubar's hugely influential *The Madwoman in the Attic*, we should not forget, and the specific issue of pornography was dividing feminists. The critic most diametrically opposed to Carter's use of Sade – and, by implication, to her ironic, 'light' re-reading of the fairy tale about the perfect woman – was Susanne Kappeler in *The Pornography of Representation*:

> Carter, the potential feminist critic, has withdrawn into the literary sanctuary, has become literary critic . . . Like good modern literary critics, we move from the author/writer to the oeuvre/text which by literary convention bears

his name ... Sade's pornographic assault on one particular patriarchal representation of woman – the Mother
– renders him, in the eyes of Carter, a provider of a
service to women ... Women, of course, neither produced
nor sanctified the mothering aspect of their patriarchal
representation, but it is doubtful whether they would thank
Sade for replacing the myth of the Mother with that of the
victim or the inverted sadist ...

Kappeler is deliberately reading Carter reductively, rather in
her own spirit; and she is wrong to suggest that Carter's
Sade *replaces* Mother with her suffering and sadist daughters
Justine and Juliette. All three, Carter argues, belong to the same
mythology (which Sade extrapolates, rather than invents): it's
Mother who makes her daughters this way, though this whole
family of women is of course also formed by patriarchal society.
What is at stake is the meaning of the 'literary': for Carter genres
like pornography, romance, fairy tale and science fiction are not
at all hedged with piety in the way Kappeler assumes. They are
already desecrating 'the literary sanctuary'. This does not mean
that they are to be claimed automatically as 'transgressive' or
'subversive', only that their currency and their craft (as opposed
to high art, except insofar as they contaminate it, which they
most often do) lend themselves to both or all parties. For Carter
does not agree with Kappeler that 'Women ... neither produced
nor sanctified the mothering aspect of their patriarchal representation'; her reading of Sade, and of fairy tales, is precisely an
attack on this version of women as blameless, as having no part in
the construction of their world, and of themselves: 'Justine marks
the start of a kind of self-regarding female masochism, a woman
with no place in the world, no status, the core of whose resistance
has been eaten away by self-pity' (*The Sadeian Woman*).

Kappeler thinks that 'representation' *in itself* is powerfully impure and voyeuristic, and therefore cannot be safely distinguished from pornography. Carter agrees. But this is where their paths diverge, for Kappeler is a fundamentalist and an iconoclast, who wants to do away with literariness, to destroy the images, and to have people speak for themselves without artifice in the name of truth. In contrast, Carter wants to turn out the mind's rumpus room and vindicate women's creative role, past and present. The blameless woman is for Carter also the unimaginative woman. So *The Sadeian Woman* and the fairy tales were a way of asserting the value of her vocation as a writer in the face of radical puritanism (compare, again, Calvino and the postwar pressure from the Party left). Not because art is autonomous: 'genre' is a site where the literary and the extra-literary confront each other and converse. Still, Carter was giving a formal, fictive and 'untruthful' answer to a political question, and that meant that, at the time, she was frequently convicted of heresy.

In the years since, the development of different emphases in gender studies has produced a theoretical frame that fits Carter so much better that it seems set to canonise her. I'm thinking, for example, of Judith Butler, with her description of bodies that 'wear' our 'cultural history' – 'the body is a *field of interpretive possibilities*, the locus of a dialectical process of interpreting anew a historical set of interpretations which have become imprinted on the flesh' ('Sex and Gender'). Butler – like Carter, though from a different angle – is spreading the act of creation around the culture at large, highlighting the symbolic importance of disguise, cross-dressing, various perverse 'carnival' tactics, as images of the not especially decadent or bohemian, but actually often *homely*, practice of making up gender as you go along. Butler's 1993 gloss on the theoretical and creative position implied in 'performativity' is a good description of Carter's procedures in *The Sadeian Woman*. 'Performativity describes this relation of being implicated in that which one opposes, this turning power against itself to produce alternative modalities of power' (*Bodies*). Fairy tales too use this tactic.

Density of allusion, quotation and bricolage were already hallmarks of Carter's writing in 1979. Some of the earlier novels are, as Elaine Jordan says, 'stories of a crucial change in some young person's life ... closer to realist fictions of experience and development'. Others are more obviously fantastical and speculative, and by the 1970s this second kind had taken over. But they shared a repertoire. Plots, for instance, tend to divide into the cabinet-of-curiosities or mausoleum shape, not quite always death-bound (*Several Perceptions* in 1968 is an open-ended exception) but essentially static; and into the more picaresque frame, with Gothic and science-fiction overtones. The girl we can recognise in retrospect as the Justine or Sleeping-Beauty type of heroine recurs again and again – murdered Ghislaine in her first novel *Shadow Dance* in 1965 and suicidal Annabel in the 1971 *Love*, but the distinction between self-murder and murder is less significant than it might seem, for this heroine lives in the passive case. In Carter's work the realist 'rite of passage' plot about the young person's entry into the world is turned ironically back on itself: this heroine's refusal to grow up is clearly for Carter the most honest and telling thing about her.

Tristessa, the Hollywood icon of *The Passion of New Eve*, is the perfection of this woman-as-idea: 'Tristessa's speciality had been suffering. Suffering was her vocation. She suffered exquisitely' (*Passion*). Her name itself, we're told, 'whispered rumours of inexpressible sadness; the lingering sibilants whispered like the doomed petticoats of a young girl who is dying'. That s/he is a transvestite makes perfect sense; indeed several of the martyred heroines are daddy's girls, his creatures. Ghislaine in *Shadow Dance*, for instance: 'You know her father's a clergyman? . . . She wrote to me that it was a spiritual defloration when I knifed her.' And Albertine in *The Infernal Desire Machines of Doctor Hoffman*, though she has many disguises, is the agent of her mad scientist father, who keeps her dead mother's body embalmed in his castle. All of these figures and more are summed up in *The Bloody Chamber* in 'The Lady of the House of Love', her strings pulled by her vampire ancestors, who sleeps all day in her coffin and sleep-walks so reluctantly through her carnivorous nights. Like her predecessors, she is 'in voluntary exile from the historic world, in its historic time that is counted out minute by minute' (*The Sadeian Woman*).[7] And that is why the prince will kill her when he wakes her up: death, though, is the one thing she's right about. The stinking red rose our hero takes from Sleeping Beauty's overgrown garden to remember her by will bloom all the way from her Transylvanian fastness to the trenches of the War in France, historic time's bloodbath.

The other implication of this story's title – the House of Love as brothel (indeed it reminds its chaste hero of a necrophiliac tableau in a brothel in Paris) – alludes shorthand-style to the bargain involved in marriage and/or prostitution. The title story 'The Bloody Chamber' refers to this, and so do the Beauty-and-the-Beast stories. *The Sadeian Woman* has a savage aphorism on the subject: '[T]he free expression of desire is as alien to pornography as it is to marriage'. This helps to explain why the heroines who survive their rite of passage are cruelly calculating, like Melanie in *Heroes and Villains*, who finds her true vocation as a widow, taking over the master's mantle – 'I'll be the tiger lady and rule them with a rod of iron'. The Little Red Riding Hood of 'The Werewolf' in *The Bloody Chamber*, who arranges for her Grandmother's murder and inherits her cottage, is in a similar mould, and so is the bride of the title story – where it's Mother who does the dirty work. In fact, these figures are now revealed as imperfect avatars of Justine's sister, Sade's Juliette:

> . . . a model for women, in some ways. She is rationality personified and leaves no single cell of her brain unused. She will never obey the fallacious promptings of her heart. Her mind functions like a computer programmed to produce two results for herself – financial profit and libidinal gratification. By the use of her reason, an intellectual apparatus women themselves are still inclined to undervalue, she rids herself of the more crippling aspects of femininity; but she is the New Woman in the mode of irony. (*The Sadeian Woman*)

New Women had been on the margins of Carter's picture since the beginning: there's a minor character, Emily, who walks away unscathed from the murderous mess at the end of *Shadow Dance*, and she does it because she's already an adept; she knows the story in advance:

> 'I found this key in one of his trouser pockets, see, and I thought, you know, of Bluebeard.'
> 'Bluebeard?'
> 'Bluebeard. And the locked room. I don't know him very well, you know. And Sister Anne, Sister Anne, what do you see . . .'

But this early character was halfway out of the book, just looking in. Carter would later in 1979 be unlocking Bluebeard's chamber from the inside.

Fairy tales, in their multiple reflections on each other, and their individual and internal layerings of interpretations, exemplify *and unravel* something of the process by which meanings get written on bodies. You can see the decorative patina – the vampire tale written over the Sleeping Beauty story, itself easily pared down to a tale as bleak and brief as 'The Snow Child' where the daughter is dreamed up and destroyed in a moment, 'nothing left of her but a feather a bird might have dropped; a bloodstain, like the trace of a fox's kill on the snow; and the rose . . .' (*The Bloody Chamber*). And in the same process, you can see *through*, see the figures and moves stripped of the weight of finality. There's no core, or point of origin, or ur-story 'underneath', just a continuous interweaving of texts. Still, there's a sense of simplification at work. You can see that mothers and stepmothers have a good deal in common; just as in Sade's text Justine and Juliette 'mutually reflect and complement one another, like a pair of mirrors' (*The Sadeian Woman*).

Doubling and redoubling these daughters, these mothers, Carter arrives, on the far side of *The Bloody Chamber*, at the virtuoso 1987 Cinderella story 'Ashputtle or The Mother's Ghost', three versions for the price of one. The first, 'The Mutilated Girls', reflects dryly on how easy it is, if you think about the stepmother's cruel urgency to marry her daughters off to the prince, to make this a tale 'about cutting bits off women, so that they will *fit in*' (*American Ghosts*), but that's to miss the agency of the (good) dead mother. Then again, Carter's narrator toys with the idea of going back into the past, where perhaps the father was already involved with the stepmother. Perhaps her daughters, too, are his? That would explain his speedy remarriage, the way that the stepfamily are dead set on replacing the first family, and the dead mother's refusal to lie down. But such a soap-opera plot 'would transform "Ashputtle" from the bare necessity of fairy tale, with its characteristic copula formula, "and then", to the emotional and technical complexity of bourgeois realism'. Instead the mothers converge: the ghost coming back to send her daughter to the ball, the stepmother hacking her daughters' feet to get them into the slipper, which after all will only fit 'Ashputtle's foot, the size of the bound foot of a Chinese woman, a stump. Almost an amputee already . . .' The ghostly mother (who's taken the form of a turtle dove) coos triumphantly, 'See how well I look after you, my darling!' Version number two, 'The Burned Child', is brief: here, there's no prince and no stepsisters, only a bare peasant drama. The ghost possesses in turn a cow, a cat and a bird and, through them, feeds her orphaned daughter, and grooms and dresses her so that she can take the man the stepmother wants: 'He gave her a house and money. She did all right.' And mother rests in peace. The third version, 'Travelling Clothes', is the shortest of all. The cruel stepmother burns the child's face; the dead mother kisses her better, gives her a red dress – 'I had it when I was your age' – and worms from her eyesockets that turn into a diamond ring ('I had it when I was your age'); the mother invites her to step into her coffin. The girl at first recoils, but the pattern is set, the formula from the past is sprung like a trap ('I stepped into *my* mother's coffin when I was your age'): 'The girl stepped into the coffin although she thought it would be the death of her. It turned into a coach and horses. The horses stamped, eager to be gone. "Go and seek your fortune, darling."'

The barer and more elliptical these stories become, however, the more they imply. We don't go back into the past realist-style to supply depth and motive; but we do go back to link the mother to *her* mother, the clothes and jewels and coach-and-horses to puberty, marriage and early death, and to link happy endings to sad ones, all of these interpretations imprinted on the flesh, here unwound like a shroud. The Lady of the House of Love wears 'a hoop-skirted dress of white satin draped here and there with lace ... [She is] a girl with the fragility of the skeleton of a moth, so thin, so frail that her dress seemed to him to hang suspended, as if untenanted in the dark air, a fabulous lending, a self-articulated garment in which she lived like a ghost in a machine' (*The Bloody Chamber*). Carter's heroines in the earlier fiction had repeatedly tried on dead women's wedding dresses, stepped into mother's shoes. They were at the same time, these stories suggest, finding out something about the nature of their skins, that those too could come off.[8]

The ghost's valediction ('Go and seek your fortune') has a double meaning, then. Either 'go and repeat the story', or 'go and *don't* repeat the story' (if you've seen the shape of mother's legacy, thanks to the story). Looking back to her novel *Love* in 1987 (itself a rewriting of her first book), Carter called it in a jokey revisionist Afterword 'Annabel's coffin' (*Love*); she herself would not repeat that structure again, though some of her characters would still act out (in freak shows, for money) the fairy tale of the perfect, suffering woman. The young person's rite-of-passage story (which fairy tale and realist fiction have conspired together to tell since the eighteenth century) is to be shed and discarded like an old skin. Or, in a different but related image – 'he gave her a house and money' – the house is burned, ruined, abandoned. Carter's characters had been burning down houses almost since the start of her writing career, and now she had worked out more exactly why: 'When mother is dead, all the life goes out of the old house. The shop in *The Magic Toyshop* gets burned down, the old dark house, and adult life begins ...' (Carter, 'Angela Carter Interviewed by Lorna Sage').

This is her farewell to 'realist fictions of experience and development', which in any case had only ever been containers for her characters' vagrant lives. She'd jettisoned a whole 'great tradition', gladly. To measure the sense of vertigo and freedom involved, you need to think back to what that tradition had meant, especially for women. Antonia Byatt, a contemporary who wants – by contrast – to salvage continuity, has described very exactly, in *Imagining Characters: Six Conversations about Women Writers*, how realist fictional structures and habits of reading work to domesticate the world: '[T]he other thing that happens in all novels is that because you read a novel by yourself in a room, inner space in your mind and outer space in novels become somehow equivalent, images of each other . . . There's a way in which the whole landscape is inside in a novel, even if it's said to be outside.'[9] The quickness and lightness of the fairy tale and the 'performative' sense of cultural history as travelling clothes all serve to undo this sense of accommodating interiority that belongs to the novel 'proper'. For Carter, outside stays out. When she moved on, post-*Bloody Chamber*, she looked to radio, film, the stage, oral and/or performance-oriented media, taking her clue from the fairy tales that cast the writer in the role of re-teller of tales.

But what is 'outside'? 'Note the absence of the husband/father' in these Cinderella stories, says the didactic narrator of 'Ashputtle': '[T]he father is unacknowledged but all the same is predicated by both textual and biological necessity. In the drama between two female families in opposition to each other because of their rivalry over men (husband/father, husband/son), the men seem no more than passive victims of their fancy, yet their significance is absolute because it is ("a rich man", "a king's son") economic' (*American Ghosts*). Carter's fictional landscapes had always been artificial (parks, gardens, the 'wilderness' itself) so that nature for her was always 'second nature', landscape history. This was father's domain. Viewed romantically, the decaying houses, cottages and castles of her novels seem to be being eaten up by nature but, if you look more closely, this nature is ready-dishevelled and stylised (by Romantics and their Victorian followers). The rose from the Vampire lady's bower can travel to France in 1914 and bloom there because historic time and fairy-tale time are linked by Father Time. In *The Infernal Desire Machines of Doctor Hoffman* (1972), the last novel with a father-magus who manipulates appearances, creating and uncreating the world, there is a minor episode with yet another doomed Sleeping Beauty, this time a waif in the landscape:

> ... the roses had quite overrun the garden and formed dense, forbidding hedges ... sprayed out fanged, blossoming whips. Those within the house were already at the capricious mercy of nature ... As I drew nearer ... I heard, over the pounding of the blood in my ears, notes of music falling ... She played with extraordinary sensitivity. The room was full of a poignant, nostalgic anguish ... her hair and dress were stuck all over with twigs and petals from the garden. She looked like drowning Ophelia. I thought so immediately, though I could not know how soon she would really drown, for she was so forlorn and desperate. A chilling and restrained passivity made her desperation all the more pathetic. (*Infernal Desire*)

For nature, read Shakespeare. When it comes to the world of outside, Carter tracks Shakespeare everywhere, for in literary terms, he is the father, and drowning Ophelia is his great kitsch contribution to the pantheon of passive heroines.[10] This reached its apogee with Victorian Sir John Everett Millais's painting of Ophelia drifting on the water, borne up by her clothes, wreathed with flowers and weeds. Carter's character Oberon in *Come unto These Yellow Sands* is meant to be lecturing on Richard Dadd's paintings inspired by *A Midsummer Night's Dream*, but cannot resist an allusion to Ophelia, for she so exactly fits his theme:

> The richly sexual symbolism of aspects of the mythology of the 'wee folk' was buried so deeply beneath the muffling layers of repression and the oppression of women . . . It might be said of these fairy painters, as Hamlet says of Ophelia:
>
> Death and affliction, even hell itself,
> She turns to favour and to prettiness. (*Yellow Sands*)[11]

Dadd's paintings (done in mental hospital after he cut his father's throat) caught, for Carter, the paralysing effects of 'burying' symbolism. Titania steps out of one of them to describe 'Dew, dew everywhere . . . the dew drips like tears that have dropped from a crystal eye, heavy, solid, mineral, glittering, unnatural' (*Yellow Sands*).[12]

These landscapes of psychohistory are for Carter, like the 'bankrupt enchantments' of fairy tales about women's passivity, true lies. That is, they can be persuaded to reveal how myths of timelessness are made and disseminated. Her 1982 story 'Overture and Incidental Music for *A Midsummer Night's Dream*', first published in the magazine *Interzone*, goes behind the scenes of Shakespeare's text in order to draw it and him into a present-tense revisionist perspective: 'This wood is, of course, nowhere near Athens; the script is a positive maze of false leads. The wood is really located somewhere in the English midlands, possibly near Bletchley, where the great decoding machine was sited. Correction . . . oak, ash and thorn were chopped down to make room for a motorway a few years ago. However, since the wood existed only as a structure of the imagination, in the first place, it will remain' (*Black Venus*). Dense layers of interpretation over time constitute this landscape, and beyond it stretch realms of pre-literary history that serve also to put it in its place – 'nothing like the dark necromantic forest in which the Northern European imagination begins and ends, where its dead and witches live, and Baba-yaga stalks about in her house with chicken's feet looking for children in order to eat them' (*Black Venus*). In the process of this narrative, Shakespeare's wood, '*the* English wood', is stripped of its nostalgic weight and universality, becomes readable and re-writable: 'there is always a way out of a maze . . . A maze is a construct of the human mind, and not unlike it . . . But to be lost in the forest is to be lost to *this* world . . .' (*Black Venus*). Shakespeare, for Carter, looks two ways; his stage was a threshold between worlds, where folk culture was made over into high culture, but never completely. In a late interview Carter observes, 'intellectuals . . . are still reluctant to treat him as popular culture . . . Shakespeare . . . is one of the great hinge-figures that sum up the past – one of the great Janus-figures that sum up the past as well as opening all the doors to the future . . . I like *A Midsummer Night's Dream* almost beyond reason, because it is beautiful and funny and camp – and glamorous and cynical . . .' (Carter, 'Angela Carter Interviewed by Lorna Sage'). Here she addresses in passing this question of the 'outside'. Shakespeare, through his connections with the pre-literary past and with popular culture past and future, points outside the very world his theatre helped construct — 'almost *beyond reason*'.

It is time to admit that, for all Carter's deconstructive and demythologising inventiveness, Marina Warner is after all right to say that her relation to fairy tales is a love-affair. It's no accident that the most popular of her tales — 'The Tiger's Bride', 'The Company of Wolves' and 'Wolf-Alice' — are those which step beyond the knowable maze. In the *Midsummer Night's Dream* story, she writes that to be lost in the forest is 'to be committed against your will — or, worse, of your own desire — to a perpetual absence from humanity, an existential catastrophe, for the forest is as infinitely boundless as the human heart' (*Black Venus*). The girls in the stories who abandon their human separateness, of their own desire (or who, like Wolf-Alice, are only now discovering it), are lovers of this mutant kind. In *The Sadeian Woman*, Carter ends with a praise of love: '[O]nly the possibility of love could awaken the libertine to perfect, immaculate terror. It is in this holy terror of love that we find, in both men and women themselves, the source of all opposition to the emancipation of women.' One could argue, I think, that the title *The Bloody Chamber* itself, alludes in the last analysis not to Bluebeard's meat-locker, nor even to the womb/tomb, but to the human heart.

My argument for fairy tales as a means of simplification and abstraction still stands, however, though I suppose it is *soul* that Carter finds so marvellously and instructively missing in them, not heart. Calvino in his essay on 'Lightness' has a phrase that applies here — 'anthropocentric parochialism' — the 'holy' difference between ourselves and the substance of the world. This 'ancient lore born on the wrong side of the blanket from religion' returns us to a world still unknown, our *profane* interiority.

Less portentously, her fairy tales returned Carter to the picaresque, time-travelling exuberance of her last two large novels, with their historical travesties, tableaus and confidence tricks which are both staged and debunked: 'The notion of a universality of human experience is a confidence trick and the notion of a universality of female experience is a clever confidence trick' (*The Sadeian Woman*). Elaine Jordan has described the double move involved here most accurately: 'Judgements of [Carter's] work have often been made from limited perspectives which ignore the extent to which she entwines the local with the global, and sees universality as something to be challenged when it's assumed as given, and constructively struggled for when it's not . . .' (Jordan). The fairy tale enabled Carter to locate and explore the processes of interpretation that make us seem ineluctably continuous with ourselves. It supplied her with an (anti-)myth of origins, a recipe for transformations, a trunkful of travelling clothes and a happy ending. Except that, as she would have been the first to object, there's no such thing, unalloyed. Her own fairy tales are exercises in the suspension of *belief*, but a glance at the snapshot of our *fin de siècle* cultural moment, presented by, for example, Elaine Showalter in *Hystories* (1997), will serve to reveal that Sleeping Beauty lives on in her dream of blamelessness.[13] Indeed, it may well be that some of the strength of Carter's present reputation is due to credulous misreading. She sometimes suspected as much: 'I become mildly irritated when people . . . ask me about the "mythic" quality of work I've written lately' (she wrote in 1983): 'I'm in the demythologising business. I'm interested in myths . . . just because they are extraordinary lies designed to make people unfree' ('Notes'). Fairy tales are less-than-myths, however. They are volatile, anybody's – 'This is how *I* make potato soup' (Carter, *Virago*, p. x). It's hard to deny for long that they are part of the historic world, and Carter's example has made it harder.

Notes

1. See 'The Savage Sideshow' for a profile by Lorna Sage. In the United Kingdom (and in Europe more generally) Carter's works are currently set texts at school and university, and the subject of a great many graduate dissertations. In 1997 she was the only contemporary British writer to be the subject of a separate seminar at the annual conference of the European Society for the Study of English (ESSE), where a large proportion of the papers focused on the fairy tales. Carter's first real fairy-tale book was her translation, *The Fairy Tales of Charles Perrault* (1979); in 1982 she edited a collection, *Sleeping Beauty and Other Favourite Fairy Tales*; *The Virago Book of Fairy Tales*, which she edited, was published in 1990; *The Second Virago Book of Fairy Tales* in 1992, the year of her death.

2. If Calvino had not at some point read Vladimir Propp he would not have written *Invisible Cities*, Carter says there of Calvino ('Angela Carter Interviewed by Lorna Sage').

3. Fevvers, the heavy-weight trapeze artiste and Winged Victory of *Nights at the Circus*, combines the characteristics of many ready-made symbolic and allegorical figures of the turn of the nineteenth century, and is subject inside the text to endless interpretation and reinterpretation. Carter and her illustrator Martin Ware had already sketched her out

in 1977 in the 'Lilac Fairy' who looks a lot like Mae West with wings in *The Fairy Tales of Charles Perrault*.

4. In this same passage Carter refers to Justine as 'the ancestress of a generation of women in popular fiction who find themselves in the same predicament, such as the heart-struck, tearful heroines of Jean Rhys, Edna O'Brien and Joan Didion who remain grumblingly acquiescent in a fate over which they believe they have no control' (*The Sadeian Woman*).

5. See Jack Zipes's essay '"Little Red Riding Hood" as Male Creation and Projection'.

6. Literature's profanity was important to Carter: 'We think blasphemy is silly', she wrote in a 1979 review of Bataille's *Story of the Eye*, 'but we're wrong' (*Expletives Deleted*). Salman Rushdie's predicament drew her deepest sympathy.

7. It may seem a bit hard to call this heroine's exile 'voluntary', though in a sense she proves it is when she abandons it, joins the world and dies.

8. In 'Donkey Skin' (*The Fairy Tales of Charles Perrault*), Carter had found a missing link for this story in the figure of the fairy godmother who sends the daughter's beautiful clothes after her: 'Wherever you may be, your trunk, with all your clothes and jewels in it, will speed after you under the ground.'

9. Byatt's 'postmodern' fictions, starting from *Possession* (1990), are actually a knowing re-creation of Victorian literary values, demystificatory neither in intent nor effect.

10. Kate Chedgzoy, in *Shakespeare's Queer Children: Sexual Politics and Contemporary Culture*, is impressed by the carnival takeover by 'illegitimate theatre' in Carter's *Wise Children*, but concentrates, for the sake of linking postcolonial themes with gay gender politics, on *The Tempest*.

11. Carter's Oberon was misquoting from memory. It is Laertes who speaks these lines, and they actually go: 'Thought and affliction, passion, hell itself . . .' (*Hamlet*, Act IV, scene 5, lines 86–87).

12. *Wise Children* (1991) stages the comic extremity of this petrified scene, on the set of the 1930s film of *A Midsummer Night's Dream*, where 'all was twice as large as life. Larger. Daisies big as your head and white as spooks, foxgloves as tall as the tower of Pisa . . . hanging in mid-air as if they'd just rolled off a wild rose or out of a cowslip, imitation dewdrops, that is, big *faux* pearls, suspended on threads. And clockwork birds, as well . . .' In this novel Tiffany, who's thought to have drowned herself but turns up alive and angry, is a New Ophelia.

13. See especially the sections on 'Recovered Memory' and 'Multiple Personality Syndrome', where Showalter, who is of course a literary critic as well as a cultural historian, finds herself describing 'stories' that have obvious fictional connections and strategies, but whose tellers absolutely refuse any suggestion that they are making them up, and indeed often 'recover' them only under hypnosis or drugs or both.

Works cited

Butler, Judith. *Bodies That Matter* (New York and London: Routledge, 1993).

——. 'Sex and Gender in Simone de Beauvoir's *Second Sex*', *Yale French Studies*, 72 (1986), 35–50.

Byatt, A. S., and Ignes Sodre. *Imagining Characters: Six Conversations about Women Writers* (London: Chatto & Windus, 1995).

Carter, Angela. *American Ghosts and Old World Wonders* (1993) (London: Vintage, 1994).

——. 'Angela Carter Interviewed by Lorna Sage', in Malcolm Bradbury and Judy Cooke (eds), *New Writing* (London: Minerva, 1992), pp. 185–93.

——. *Black Venus* (London: Chatto & Windus, 1985).

——. *The Bloody Chamber* (1979) (London: Vintage, 1995).

——. *Come unto These Yellow Sands: Four Radio Plays* (Newcastle on Tyne: Bloodaxe, 1985).

——. *Expletives Deleted: Selected Writings* (1992) (London: Vintage, 1993).

——. *The Fairy Tales of Charles Perrault* (London: Gollancz, 1977).

——. *Heroes and Villains* (1979) (Harmondsworth: Penguin, 1981).

——. *The Infernal Desire Machines of Doctor Hoffman* (1972), rpt. *The War of Dreams* (New York: Bard/Avon Books, 1977; Harmondsworth: Penguin, 1982).

——. Interview, by William Bedford, *New Yorkshire Writing*, 3 (Winter 1978), 1–2.

——. *Love* (1971) (rev. edn., London: Chatto & Windus, 1987).

——. 'Notes from the Front Line', in *Gender and Writing*, ed. Michelene Wandor (London: Pandora, 1983), pp. 69–77.

——. *The Passion of New Eve* (1977) (London: Virago, 1982).

——. *The Sadeian Woman: An Exercise in Cultural History* (London: Virago, 1979).

——, ed., *The Second Virago Book of Fairy Tales* (London: Virago, 1992).

——. *Shadow Dance* (1965) (London: Virago, 1994).

——, ed., *Sleeping Beauty and Other Favourite Fairy Tales* (London: Gollancz, 1982).

——. *The Virago Book of Fairy Tales* (London: Virago, 1990).

——. *Wise Children* (London: Chatto & Windus, 1991).

Chedgzoy, Kate. *Shakespeare's Queer Children; Sexual Politics and*

Contemporary Culture (Manchester: Manchester University Press, 1995).

Dundes, Alan, ed., *Little Red Riding Hood: A Casebook* (Madison: University of Wisconsin Press, 1989).

Jordan, Elaine. 'The Dangerous Edge', in Sage, *Flesh and the Mirror*, pp. 189–215.

Kappeler, Susanne. *The Pornography of Representation* (Oxford: Polity, 1986).

Sage, Lorna, ed., *Flesh and the Mirror: Essays on the Art of Angela Carter* (London: Virago, 1994).

———. 'The Savage Sideshow', *New Review*, 4: 39–40 (July 1977), pp. 51–7.

Showalter, Elaine. *Hystories* (London: Picador, 1997).

Vonnegut, Kurt. *Palm Sunday* (London: Jonathan Cape, 1981).

Warner, Marina. 'Angela Carter: Bottle Blonde, Double Drag', in Sage, *Flesh and the Mirror*, pp. 243–56.

Zipes, Jack. *Breaking the Magic Spell: Radical Theories of Folk and Fairy Tales* (London: Heinemann, 1979).

———, ed., *Don't Bet on the Prince* (New York: Methuen, 1986).

———. '"Little Red Riding Hood" as Male Creation and Projection', in Dundes, *Little Red Riding Hood*, pp. 121–8.

PERMISSIONS